F*CK THE ODDS

How to Bet on You, and WIN!

Ernest Fenton

Contents

Preface

In *The Soul of Black Folk*, W.E.B. Du Bois exclaimed that America's greatest dilemma was that of the Color Line. Considering history's propensity to repeat itself in some manner, if that were true in 1969, I contend that the dilemma of today's America is outlined by the onslaught of college graduates solemnly standing in the *unemployment or underemployment line*. Adding to that reality is the crisis caused by student loan debt, circling above society's heads with the menacing hunger of a scavenging vulture. This infamous monster ventures off on a tireless quest, in hopes of devouring any unsuspecting prey with the misfortune of landing in its path. Lurking in the distance, preparing to pounce, that dreaded loan monster whispers out into the distance, "Default if you dare. One slipup is all it takes— you will be mine forever. There is no escaping my grasp. I will own all your hopes, dreams, and accomplishments."

Essentially, Sallie Mae and other student loan giants demand that you sign your life away in blood. For those who don't believe me, I now present Exhibit A: former President Barack Obama.

The nation's beloved 44th Commander in Chief was still saddled with student loan debt as he presided as State Senator and Congressman. In 2012, he addressed a collegiate audience of voters at the University of North Carolina at Chapel Hill and made a cringing confession.

"I'm the president of the United States. We only finished paying off our student loans about eight years ago. That wasn't that long ago."

To the group, Obama made light of the fact he was finally able to pay off his student loan debt when he was provided a book advance in 2004. Between the earnings received from his memoir, *Dreams from My Father*, his salary from the senate, and the paycheck Michelle accumulated as an executive with the University of Chicago Hospital, the political powerhouse couple reported a combined income of $204,647. Even after serving on the senate for seven years, and serving on a number of professional boards, Barack Obama still had outstanding student loan debt four years prior to becoming President of the United States of America. It took about a decade for the couple to pay them off, and, if it hadn't been for the advance on his book, it may have taken much longer.

The country's first couple was still paying off student loan debt at 40 and 42! Can you believe that? For so many, the student loan plague has become a waking nightmare that carries the essence of a Stephen King -Tyler Perry hybrid film. What's that mean? We don't know whether we should be terrified, laughing, or crying.

If the student loan debt crisis-monster-plague-dilemma isn't enough to make your stomach churn, let's talk about yet another debate that's turned our country on its axle. The Baby Boomer Epidemic. In this sense, the "greying" of America is more than a reference to hair color. It is also the color of the economic cloud cast above the heads of many doomed to find themselves to be living in one of society's most controversial generations. It's ironic to witness baby boomers become victims of their own beliefs in the American Dream. The same Social Security and pension systems previously coveted by this generational group have now become the subjects of discontent and injustice.

You should also keep in mind that, with Social Security being at the top of the list amongst heated political debates, it's extremely likely that you may face a depressing bounty—if you ever receive a check. If you believe the pundits, the Social Security system is on the verge of breakdown. At the very least, we're living in a world where one out of every four retirees confessed that their Social Security checks are smaller than expected. As it stands, the rubric is designed to supplement about 40% of your income, but that's not the case for everyone. In fact, if you're retiring in 2018, you'll need to make less than $895 per month to receive credit for 90% of your income. Anyone who earns $895 up to the cap of $5,397 will only walk away with a 32% credit. Rates drop down to 15% for anyone who makes more than the median limit. Essentially, Social Security policies *penalize* those who are more successful. So where does that leave you?

There is a parallel dilemma to Social Security existing with pensions. While many debate against the reality of a clear-cut "pension crisis", one can't deny that, overall, pension plans just aren't what they once were. First and foremost, they're rapidly disappearing from employee benefit packages everywhere. No matter which of these evils you choose to confront, it's become inherently clear that the American workforce is being left to fend for themselves. Are you prepared to wield your sword?

Since few are prepared to face the unsettling reality of retirement abandonment, many retirees are waking up to a shocking post-work apocalypse. Seniors, by default, deserve to be the benefactors of a comfortable lifestyle; one that carries them throughout their golden years. As the most advanced society in this era of mankind, if we can't ensure that—at the very least—then we seriously need to re-assess our definition of advanced.

Let's take a break from the doom and gloom delivery, just for a minute. I don't want to solely be the bearer of bad news—there's something to gain, if we choose to look at the glass as half-full. Anyone who's fortunate enough to be a

Baby Boomer in today's economic climate has what I call "a good dilemma".

What's so good about it?

Long life and endless opportunity! In 2018, the average life expectancy is greater than it has ever been in the history of mankind. In the United States, men and women are estimated to live to the ripe average age of 79. Many seniors are living productive and fun filled lifestyles; they're redefining what's awaiting on the other side of the retirement gates. There are so many exceptional tales of our elders performing remarkable feats. I see it so often I quickly realized that it was time for me to adjust my perception and accept that "senior" doesn't automatically equate a life bound to front porches and rocking chairs, like society would have you believe. Any remnant of doubt remaining dissipated when this happened:

Ring, ring!

After checking the time on my cell phone, I realized it's about 11:30 p.m. Friday night. Why in the world would my mother be calling me? "It must be an emergency!" I thought to myself.

Anxious, yet reluctant, I hesitantly pressed accept.

"Hello?" I said as I answered the phone.

"Are you home?" my mother quickly questioned.

"Yes," I replied, with a hundred questions and concerns whirling through my head.

"Well, I'm out with some friends and left my wallet at home. I'm stopping by. I need you to give me some money."

I was done!

Are you serious? There I was, sitting home alone on a weekend. I'm sound asleep while my "senior" of a mother was out having a good time with her friends. From that point forward, it was official. My life was headed downhill.

You can imagine why I've been too embarrassed to tell this story, until now. My mother's bustling social life made me question my own. Was I a nerd? Had I lost my mojo? Was she Mrs. Congeniality and I was doomed to be a lone wolf? I'll admit, she had me doubting myself for a quick moment. Fortunately, I've since moved on.

All embarrassing confessions aside, my point is, old age and long life has fashioned itself into a double-edged sword. While we should be celebrating this momentous achievement afforded to us through health and longevity, we must acknowledge the grim duality that comes along with it too. Not all are privy to health and vitality in their later years. There are many who must manage the burden of depreciating lifestyles that have fallen victim to rising health care costs, an inadequate and hemorrhaging Social Security system, and evaporating pension plans.

What originated as the Color Lined dilemma spotlighted by Du Bois has evolved into an American class dilemma. On one side, there's the 1% of the population (some reports have reduced the figure to 0.7%) that controls approximately 50% of the wealth. Surprisingly enough, the Great Recession of 2008 somehow stimulated a consistent increase in this group's fiscal control. Rising from 42.5% to 50% in the last decade, this has created the greatest financial divide our country has experienced in the past 50 years. Let that sink in for a minute: 50% of the wealth in America is controlled by the top 1% of the population.

This is an appalling widening of the wealth gap between the proverbial "haves and have-nots." This economic imbalance is fueling a discontent and distrust between the working and "figurative" ruling class.

We can recall the outcry and march on Wall Street dated back in 2009. It was a forewarning sent off by the euphemistic ninety-nine percenters in response to the very epidemic we're enduring right now. Eternally stamped in history, it is an inspiring display of solidarity between eclectic middle America. Amongst the outraged were people of all characteristics. Short and tall. Black and white. Blue collar and white collar, working men and women.

As a somewhat political cynic, I must admit I was thoroughly inspired by this moment. I'd go as far as to say this moment took me a step further than mere "inspiration"; it left me hopeful that a systemic change was forthcoming. It riled me up in anticipation of the birth of a new nation state; representative of the demands of the people and not the "ruling class."

We are the 99%, the overwhelming majority. The time has come for us to learn how to proactively pursue our own liberation, rather than idly reacting to the crumbs left over after feasts held by gluttonous one-percenters.

The urgency of this moment has created yet another pressing dilemma. The ruling class comfortably sits back as they search for ways to reconcile the ideals of American Democracy and Capitalism. The population is already bound by the unbearable shackles of credit card and student loan debt. Recurring servitude paves the way for starved citizens to work themselves to the bone, only to be met by ineffective Social Security and pension systems. The effects of this economical divide spill over into our communities, threatening the safety of our neighborhoods, offering unequal access to technology, and limited educational opportunities. These congested "democratic" ideals struggle to see the light beyond the shadows cast by a criminal and judicial system that can be unevenly weighted in the favor of capitalist benefit. With that being said, the people have more power than we immediately acknowledge.

I know what you're thinking. Doom's Day statistics and underwhelming prophecies aren't necessarily your idea of an entertaining read. Before you turn your head away, bear with me for a minute. Now that we've let a few fiscal skeletons out of the closet, I can lay the foundation for the powerful story to come. I promise it gets better later; just hold on for a while longer.

In the meantime, I need you to allow me to get it all out. Nobody likes to talk about the elephant in the room, but that won't stop him from squashing you.

I need you to forgive me, please, because I'm literally laughing out loud right now. I just can't contain myself. I can remember once upon a time when the sheer thought of being responsible for my financial future literally drove me mad. To be clear, I'm laughing with you right now. You may not get the joke just yet, but you will by the time you've completed this book. How can I be so sure? I've been there before.

I promise, *I get it.* Thankfully, I've found my way after trekking along an arduous journey of success and self-discovery. Today, I can laugh with you because I've figured out a better release for the tears I've cried in the past. Tears I know still stain the cheeks of many of my readers.

Let me start by saying, "It's ok!" Nothing is ever exactly as it seems. If you picked up this book in hopes of finding a solution to a pressing economic dilemma—you should be jumping for joy, because you've just treated yourself to a resource that can turn your entire life around *forever.*

They say the first step to recovery is admitting there's a problem.

Fine. "Houston, we have a problem!"

I said it for the both of us. Now, hopefully, we can move on.

Yet, here we are. Seven years later, the same nation that gave me so much hope through its powerful demand for equality elected a self-indulged, gaudy, gold-toilet-seat-installing, billionaire named Donald Trump as its president. Remember those tears of joy I spoke of earlier? Now, they've become disgruntled cries of pain and anguish.

Even with a heart filled with disappointment and disgust, what's done is done. The results of our 45th presidential election is a truth we'll all have to accept—for now. Since we've spent some time bonding, laughing and crying together, I guess I'll let you in on a little about the man behind the madness.

Chapter 1

Introduction

Allow me to introduce myself:

I am Ernest B. Fenton. The 'B' is for Brandon. Seven seven seventy (7-7-70). That's my birthday. July 7th, 1970. Born the fourth child of a total of six between Ruby and Red Fenton. Well, I am actually my father's namesake. His first name is Ernest too.

I can trace my earliest childhood memory back to the age of two. I remember pushing the heavy door of the bathroom open in our three-bedroom one-bath apartment on the Southside of Chicago. I was being trained at an early age to sit on the pot or find yourself wet. Yes. My first memories are of potty training or, as I later realized, my first boot camp. Better yet, poop camp—and the training got real.

I'd pull my diaper down, take a seat on the pot strategically placed under the shelves behind the door and proudly accomplish what I set out to do. I always thought that moment was simply a marker of my first memory. In speaking of it now, I realize it also marks my first conscious encounter with success. From two years old and on, life taught me one recurring lesson:

Success is a Muscle that must be Exercised Consciously and Often

---

We lived on the third floor of a low-rise project called Madden Park. The staircase was oftentimes dominated by the smell of urine. The kitten-size rats would patrol the dark staircase to gather scraps from the litter. Despite those obstacles, it really didn't seem too bad. In fact, most of my memories are of laughter and good times. Tonka trucks being pushed through the mud puddles we called a playground. Front and backward flips on stained mattresses found propped against the big green garbage cans. Rock fights, running contests, and makeshift baseball games of "strike out" against the side of the building.

There were certain days and times we had to leave the park because the gangs would call a meeting. We'd simply retreat to a safe distance and wait patiently until their meeting was adjourned. It's amazing how a person can adapt and normalize circumstances that would completely destabilize another.

Reflecting on my childhood, I can recall hearing gunshots at night—ducking and hoping none ripped through my home.

"Get away from the window boy! What's wrong with you? Close that window right now," my eldest sister, Maranda, would chastise me for my innocent curiosity.

I never really knew we were considered poor or, perhaps, simply "lower class" citizens. I just knew I was never hungry. I slept on the top bunk of the bunk bed shared by my older brother, Malcolm. Even if it wasn't much, we had all that we needed.

I knew when the skies darkened and street lights illuminated it meant it was time to go inside. I knew the tall buildings across the street and the areas where my cousins lived were considered much worse than our apartment complex. We were in the "well to do" area of the "ghetto." An oxymoron in itself.

In late spring of 1976, I remember loading a truck parked at the bottom of our building. We were carrying boxes, lamps with big round globes, my parents bull and matador, and the picture that you plugged in at night to watch it light up. I didn't know where we were going. I was only told we were moving. I'd be leaving my friends, the park, my school, and all of what I knew. But what I didn't know, was the lessons I learned at such an early age would shape much of who I would become—a story I'll continue to share in the pages to come.

I never could've imagined that life would've taken me down the pathway I've journeyed over the years. From the projects to the suburbs. From the military to retail sales. Real estate to practicing law; Radio talk show host to author. I'm still in awe of what can be accomplished with a bit of focus and motivation.

It seems like a lot. I'm tired from just reading it. Would I be crazy to say that I feel like I'm still not done? That, even with all I've achieved, there's still more for Ernest B. Fenton?

Would you believe that I didn't know I had a middle name until I was about five years old? I can remember the day I realized I had another name as vividly as if it were yesterday's news.

I sat staring out the bedroom window, pondering on how it was possible for me to have a name I never knew. Aunt Tina, visiting from St. Louis, called out to me using this unfamiliar title. It was doubly strange that she called me this "new" name speaking in such an odd accent. It took some time, but I later learned that having a middle name wasn't uncommon at all. (However, I'm still not convinced people from St. Louis do not sound strange when they talk.)

Ok, on to more important matters…

My inspiration for writing this book.

I have travelled along many roads in a relatively brief period of time. Like many others, my journey has been filled with considerable hardships and challenges, as well as a collection of exceptionally satisfying accomplishments. Along the way, my feats have taught me invaluable lessons. As any good steward and student of life, I am not only required, but also inspired, to give to you as much of what I know in the pages to follow.

"to whom much is given, much is required."

I must admit, I've developed quite the resume for myself. Professionally, I am a practicing attorney in the Chicagoland area. My primary practice centers around the areas of estate planning, real estate, and business affairs. I was a driving force during the Great Recession of 2009, as I represented thousands of families in foreclosure hearings.

I've watched grown men break down from the fear of losing the property they and their families called home. I've had to make the difficult call to a single mother to inform her of the foreclosure sale of her house. I watched as the banks were provided trillions of dollars through stimulus packages while the middle class was left to fend for itself.

Although the worst of the Great Recession is behind us (for now), the remnants of the crisis remain. Homes have been stripped of their equity. Retirement accounts are still struggling to replenish. Small businesses have yet to fully recover from such a destructive hit.

Overcoming the lingering winds of the recession won't come about easily, especially if you aren't armed with the knowledge and skills needed to bounce back from the blow.

4

I am sharing my story but, essentially, these words are meant for *you.*

You, the young African American man birthed into humble beginnings that left you questioning the possibilities offered to you in this world.

You, the high school student who struggled to meet academic performance requirements which left you doubtful of your future.

You, the single mother concerned about the life she'll leave behind for her child, if ever the unexpected unfolds.

And *you*, Baby Boomer who has earned your stripes, happily retired and enjoying a mortgage-free lifestyle. I know many of you may worry about the cash you've saved, but I'll show you how to prosper over the long term—just trust me.

This book, this guide, stands as a tool that contains something for all of you—me. Ernest B. Fenton. Graduate of Harvard Law School and, more importantly, son of Ernest "Red" Fenton and Ruby Mae Fenton. Life taught me to accept the unexpected from an early age. My parents instilled a wealth of knowledge and values in me that carried me through the most challenging trials of my career. Now that I'm here, enjoying what I know to be but a temporary glimpse of success, I've taken an oath to use all I've learned to benefit someone else.

And so, it begins. Are you ready?

Chapter 2

From the Cradle to the Grave

It was a bright day back in March or April 2014. Clear skies and the first signs of spring surfacing made it a prime opportunity to take a relaxed 30-minute drive to neighboring Schaumburg, IL. Schaumburg is an Apple Pie and Ice Cream all-American northern suburb of Chicago. My specific destination? One of the greatest present day inventions birthed from our generation—IKEA.

It's one of those things that balance the universe, for me. IKEA is a place where young and old, black and white, trust fund and "borrowed some" can all convene to enjoy a brief moment of mutual understanding.

Bargain shopping and bliss. What more could you ask for?

On this particular day, I was on the hunt for white and red picture frames to decorate my condo. As I ferreted through the frame section, I was distracted by a family shopping in the same area. First, Papa Bear caught my attention. A classically clad 30-something Caucasian man donning a cardigan sweater and flanked wool coat with a matching scarf. He definitely looked like an IKEA frequent flyer. Then, I noticed his impeccable wife toting along with two adventurous children in tow. From the outside looking in, they appeared to be your average family. That is, before the unthinkable happened.

Like most multi-child households, the children were actively engaging in an improv-worthy cry for attention. This round, it seemed as if the eldest of the two was dominating the arena with his tactfully delivered five-year-old demands. The preschooler was persistently making his argument in favor of his right to purchase, *at least*, a few items within his grasp.

Mama Bear seemed quite patient and accustomed to her son's propositions. Even his best efforts weren't enough to sway or aggravate her. Occasionally, she'd dismiss his requests with a simple, "You can't have that" or "No, please put that down". Even with her passive objections, our miniature debater wasn't prepared to throw in the towel.

Papa Bear, on the other hand, took a much different approach. He didn't appear to be as amused by the little one's determined approach. Operating from an obvious variant in tolerance levels, dad was the one who delivered the stern "NO!" With a penetrating glare, he slowly repeated himself, "I said NO. Don't ask anymore."

Here's the part where we take bets. What do you think Junior did next?

If your guess was "stand his ground for several more minutes" then you, my friend, hit the nail on the head! To think, I'm the one who went to law school, but this little fella gave his parents a run for their money. Surprisingly enough, that statement manifested in a much more literal sense than you may have considered.

Eventually, the back and forth debates and landslide negotiations ended with this impressive tike throwing the gauntlet down on his dad. He was clearly building up to a public tantrum. Before the little guy seized the moment completely, his father responded with, "Fine! If you want that, then place it in the cart. But, if we buy it, we're going to use *your* money from *your* account."

Now, typically I'm not one to eavesdrop or stick around for too long but, first off, it's IKEA, the land of milk and honey—and, secondly, I was floored!

Imagine me there, standing in the aisle, doing my best to shuffle between armloads of bargain picture frames, while working even harder to tone down my laughter. My ears couldn't believe what they just heard. Your money. Your account. Was that supposed to be some sort of a threat?

At first, I thought, is this really what the world has come to? Is this our little persuader's greatest burden? To have the money drawn from his account—to purchase a few "just because" picture frames to house his stick figure drawings?

Excuse me if I'm a little out of the loop, or if I've missed something during the last decade or two but, who put that money in his account in the first place? Does this kid have a job or something?

Last I checked there were child labor laws in effect and sweatshops were banned across the globe. Unless our budding Picasso was a baby genius or something, weren't those parents essentially punishing themselves?

In that moment, something else occurred to me too. Well, *reoccurred*, if I'm being completely honest. It was then that I was struck with the revelation that there are significant disparities between the ways some children are raised.

When I was young, I had to negotiate a 50-cent bomb pop from the ice cream truck. Hearing the hypnotic sounds of the ice cream truck on a hot Saturday afternoon elicited mixed emotions in me.

I was uncontrollably excited and fearful at the same time. Maybe this is what the young guy was experiencing at IKEA. Comedian Eddie Murphy in his 1983 standup special, *Delirious*, parodied the pain of thousands of children who, like me, had panic attacks upon hearing the majestic sounds of the bells signaling the oncoming of the ice cream truck.

As Eddie said, no matter what I was doing, once I heard the ice cream truck, I would dart in the house to make a desperate plea for any loose change my parents had. My mother might say, "I don't have any change, ask your father. My father might say, 'boy, get out of here. You always asking me for something.'" I knew, just like the kid in IKEA, this was simply the beginning of the negotiation. There was no way I'd allow the ice cream truck to escape me!

"It's fifty cents! I need fifty cents! I can't have ice cream. Hurry Up. He's leaving." I'd exclaim. It's hilarious to think back. Catching that ice cream truck was an emergency to me. I was clearly "extra" in that moment. Again, just like the little guy in IKEA.

I learned a valuable lesson early on. Ice cream is not free; hilarious. And, you best be ready when the ice cream man drives down your block.

Now, I'm looking at this youngster standing ten toes down in IKEA negotiating a $15 picture frame for his own leisure. There is, of course, an almost 40-year difference in time between us. Even still, I hardly doubt that inflation can drastically lessen the difference between the value of the objects we each desired.

With that being said, this kid was clearly light-years ahead of me in terms of financial literacy. His ability to respond to rebuttals from his parents concerning banking and personal accounts far superseded my comprehension as a child. Let alone *his* bank account.

Dare I confess the fact that I did not open (or even consider having) a bank account until I enlisted in the military? In my senior year of high school at age 17, my mother took me to a local bank to open my first bank account. Prior to reporting for basic training, I needed to have a bank account so my checks could be directly deposited. This was my first experience with a bank account. By the time the IKEA child is 17, he'll probably have a retirement account in order.

Of course, that's merely speculation, but one thing's for sure—he'll have a head start over many of his peers.

The bank account. What a phenomenal invention!

Just the thought of how many doors this underrated phenomenon can open strikes a eureka moment within my soul. Can you imagine what could come from using bank accounts as the cornerstone of early childhood education across the world?

Where would our youth find themselves, on both a general and literal level, if they were introduced to financial literacy as early as Pre-K or Kindergarten? We already encourage children to learn to count; wouldn't counting money serve as an enticing incentive? Even for a five-year-old—I mean, listen to that kid's negotiating skills.

No matter where you find yourself on the planet, money will stand as the most universally recognized language. Coast to coast. Sea to sea. Continent to continent. Money is the root to humanity's advancement.

I'd go as far as to suggest that basic banking should be included as a prerequisite to kindergarten graduations. Why shouldn't we level the playing field?

Children like my IKEA hero are negotiating payment alternatives while, somewhere out there, another child doesn't have any clue about what a bank account is.

Our school systems love to push "No Child Left Behind" manifestos but, if we really want to guarantee that each child is afforded equal opportunity, we must begin with the knowledge and understanding that forms the foundation for their entire adult experience. Seeds are planted in our children from the second they exit the womb; why shouldn't we work to ensure that these seeds will one day bear financially abundant fruit?

Foundation is key in any type of construction. Even when we're dealing with construction of one's consciousness, we must always consider the foundation.

Sure, banking and financial accounts may seem like a commonplace addition to the average working adult's world, but you'd be surprised by how many legal-aged people understand as much about money as I did when I was begging for that bomb pop.

Let's take an example like Allen Iverson, a very talented player in the 90s era of the National Basketball Association. Though he was widely revered as a prolific point guard who scored with a surgeon's precision, he'll always be remembered for his exclamation to the press:

"Practice. You're talking about practice?"

The narrative in the press and among the public, is Iverson mistakenly thought he was dismissing criticism from the coach and the public because he religiously missed practice. He felt like skipping out on potential team-building opportunities and staggered underperformance wasn't an issue. Iverson believed that his grandeur during game time should've overshadowed any lack of team spirit. His words pushed one message, but the point he really conveyed was that he was astoundingly clueless when it came to the significance of practice.

Iverson was caught up on his natural talent so much that he forced himself to rest at an athletic plateau. What he missed was that practice is where other players gain confidence and critical skills. Practice is the place where chemistry is created amongst your team members. Practice builds trust and mutual understanding.

Practice time may have seemed futile for a player with such prized raw skills but, in reality, it is where we have an opportunity to learn, grow, and use mistakes as the building blocks for future greatness. Allen Iverson thought it absurd for anyone to place so much stock on "practice," but he missed the mark.

Now, let's consider how this same dismissiveness can impact a person on a financial level. Over Iverson's 15-year career, he earned over $200 million, yet there were still rumors circulated of him nearing bankruptcy upon retiring his jersey. Of course, there are many reasons why someone may file for federal financial relief. To be objective, Iverson denounced claims of his spendthrift behaviors; while others claim Reebok was his only saving grace. Whether it was due to gambling addictions, the costly expense of maintaining a 50-piece entourage, or simply celebrity folklore, would the NBA's crossover poster child have been afforded a greater advantage had he been instilled with the knowledge of financial management from an early age?

A bank account is a great "practice" ground to teach financial literacy. I sincerely believe it's as essential as the Tonka Truck was for me or a doll is for many young girls. Some may dismiss the suggestion as completely absurd. "A bank account for a five-year-old?" Yes! That's my story and I'm sticking to it.

No, I don't mean a secondary account for the parent to stuff away a loose $50 bill until their child stomps his feet for an ice cream cone. I mean an introduction into the importance of money management.

Kids today are like supercomputers, compared to what we were back in the day. Don't believe me? Hand your phone over to a preschooler and see how quickly they make their way to YouTube or, even better, begin downloading their favorite games from the App Store.

Today's kids are ready to grasp money management concepts early than we were. It's never too early to begin teaching our children. Education must begin as early as the cradle. It will become the foundation for knowledge and understanding children will take to their graves

I'm no A.I., and I certainly wasn't raised with the privileges offered to our IKEA maverick, but I can recall a few childhood lessons of my own.

McDonald's Changed My Life

There are certain sacred experiences every child in America born pre-1990 has experienced. This right of passage is as sacred as bar mitzvah for a thirteen-year-old Jewish child; obtaining your driver's license at sixteen; senior year prom; and high school graduation, combined. Yes, combined. The most troublesome child has been known to instantaneously convert to an angel child on this day. Sweet mild-mannered children have been known to lose their cool upon approach. What do you ask, am I speaking of?

Adorned across the sky all across America are what was heaven's gateway for school age children in the early eighties, affectionately known as the Golden Arches. The threat or promise of McDonald's in the eighties has been replaced by the iPhone. Some of my most memorable childhood memories involved McDonald's. Like the time the car rolled onto my foot in the parking lot. Like the time I had three dollars and McDonald's had Big Macs on sale for two for one dollar. And, like the time my mother, father, and, I believe, two siblings, were returning home from my parents' friend's home. I recall driving down 159th street in Markham; my heart gently palpitating. I had an internal prayer chant, "if there is truly a God, my father will pull this car into McDonald's. Please. Please." I can hear my mother, "what are we going to eat? We can just go to McDonald's!" Oh my...it's going to happen. It HAPPENED!

Here's how it went down. We were allowed no special requests. You see, my mother was a mind reader, like many of yours. Thus, there was no need to ask.

My mother, "We'll have eight cheeseburgers, 4 orders of small french fries and 4 small coca colas." Not all of what I wanted, but I'll take it. Reflecting back, it's quite amazing my parents were able to splurge on five children and themselves at McDonald's.

But, my greatest McDonald's moment had nothing to do with french fries, cheeseburgers, and not even my favorite, caramel sundaes with extra nuts. It all started on a sunny summer day. My childhood best friend's mother, and my surrogate second mother, Ms. Smith, decided to treat us to McDonald's. We had gone to the local grocery store and McDonald's was a brisk ten minute walk away. I can actually recall our approach. The Golden Arches beckoning us as we walked through the half-barren blacktop-paved parking lot.

Now we're standing in front of the counter. Ms. Smith is standing closest to the counter; my friend standing off to the side and somewhat behind his mother. I'm standing a couple of steps behind his mother. Not quite certain if I should approach. Was she going to "just" order for us all? Was she too a mindreader like my mother?

Then, she looks over at her son, "What do you want to order?" Then it began. He said, "I want a Big Mac with cheese. A large order of french fries. A large Coke. A strawberry sundae with nuts and an Apple Pie." I literally almost passed out. I had never imagined such an order.

Then it was my turn. She looked back at me and said, "Ditto. What would you like?" I was nervous. In my head, I wanted everything he just ordered. But, something inside of me would not allow me to articulate my fantasy order. So, I calmed my nerves, and softly replied, "A cheeseburger." Yes. I said, "a cheeseburger." She paused and then asked, "would you like french fries?" I paused again, "yes." She said, "what size?" My mind was screaming large, but my disobedient mouth said, "a medium." She said to the cashier, "he'll have a cheeseburger and a medium order of french fries." Then she looked back over at me and said, "what would you like to drink?" I paused, and then it came, one of the most pivotal moments of my life. On this day I was taught an invaluable lesson that has served me since. And something that is ingrained in my psyche forever.

Ms. Smith said sternly, "Boy. I brought you here to order food. You can have whatever you want. IF SOMEONE ASKS YOU WHAT YOU WANT, YOU TELL THEM!" On that day, I was forever changed. Standing in front of the cashier at McDonald's. In that moment I got that it is ok to ask for what you desire. That little boy at IKEA clearly understood that concept. Perhaps his delivery needs to be developed, but asking for his desires, he has that mastered.

"...When Someone Asks What You Want, Tell Them..."

In college, my fourth year paper was on the correlation between expectations and achievement. My research supported my hypothesis of the positive correlation between what a person expects and what they achieve. The greater an individual's expectation, the greater likelihood of achievement. I have bought into the idea of articulating my desires to the Universe with the expectation of the Universe responding or fulfilling my requests.

You have not, because you ask not.

I think what separates many people is not their ability, intelligence, or opportunity. The defining characteristic or factor oftentimes is one person simply asking and expecting more. More from themselves. More from others. More from life.

As children we are taught, in subtle and not so subtle ways, of our boundaries. As adults, these boundaries in the workplace are called glass ceilings. As women, these boundaries are institutionalized by sexism and internal restrictions based upon gender. As an African American male, these boundaries show up in the justice system, where many of us expect to receive less than fair and equitable justice. Well, Ms. Smith told me to ask for what I want. So, when I enter the courtroom, I expect to win when the law is on my side. I expected to gain admission into a top tier law school and do well academically. It doesn't matter if the outcome does not always align with my expectations. She never said I would receive all that I ordered. She just said, "when someone asks you what you want, you tell them."

She also never said, "who is the someone asking." So, I became the someone. I ask myself the most important questions.

Who are you going to be in this world?

How great can you actually become?

How many other countries would you like to visit?

How much money do you want to make?

How old do you want to be when you retire?

What type of relationship do you want with your spouse?

I didn't always realize the impact of that moment. Also, I'm sure it was a combustible moment; an explosion created by thousands of micro lessons coming together and exploding in my mind. I think Oprah, calls it the "aha moment."

What if we intentionally set out to teach young people the lessons of the young man at IKEA: personal responsibility and budgeting. With the lesson of Ms. Smith: understanding the possibility of your desires being met if you'd only ask. Oh, and the lesson of my youth: be grateful for what you have, because no matter how unfortunate a circumstance you find yourself in, there's almost always someone in worse straits.

Chapter 3

Is the Fifteen-Year-Old You Controlling Your Life?

I only had four pair of pants. As a middle-schooler approaching the height of his social prime, you can only imagine how that made me feel. Well, I had a few other options to choose from but, of them all, only about four were "acceptable."

Remember, this was middle school. The time of our lives when we first begin to train ourselves to really care about what others think. With four pair of pants, it was excruciatingly difficult for me to uphold my budding reputation, but I made do.

I had to learn to be strategic throughout the 7th and 8th grade. It took acute attention to detail to decide how to get away with wearing the same pair of pants twice in the same week. Would I start with one wear on Monday, then switch things up with a different top? Would Tuesday be a better day to kick off the cycle? If, Tuesday, then I'd wear them again Thursday or Friday. Never two days in a row. And the following week, I'd wear a different pair twice. Whatever I did, the last thing I needed was to create a pattern that would force me to wear the same pants back to back.

I'd wash whichever pair I was wearing a second time in the sink the night before. Hang them to dry on a hanger in the summer or lay them on the floor by the heat vent on a towel in the winter. If, for whatever reason, they weren't dry, I'd turn on the oven and place them on the oven door for a few minutes. Flipping them over periodically. Clean?

Check. Ironed? Check. I'd take a few glances in the mirror and make my way to school.

Although I adapted, I must say this strained reality picked away at my prepubescent pride, but, for what it's worth, I made it work for as long as I could.

I never considered myself unfortunate, although it certainly was a source of discontent and uneasiness. Overall, however, it was just something I had to do.

The 1985 Tinley Park High School Boycott

The summer of '85 struck me by surprise. Approaching the crest of my sophomore year in high school, my 15-year-old self was thrilled about the idea of going back-to-school shopping. It was an annual ritual that I conditioned myself to believe was to be expected throughout my school years. It was as old a tradition for me as was eating cornflakes and watching cartoons on a Sunday morning. It was held as sacred as my belief in Bruce Lee being the toughest man in the world. I mean, what was there to think about!

I'm sure you remember your sophomore year, don't you? No longer a freshman, you're a little more established in the social sphere—seasoned, to say the least. In middle school, I managed to get away with meticulously rotating my clothes but in high school that was out of the question. C'mon, we all remember how fashion-forward society was in the 80s. Everyone took pride in stepping out the house in the freshest gear. With the summer coming to an end, I became anxious after realizing that my mother still hadn't taken me school shopping. In fact, she never mentioned anything about it.

My mind was fixated on our old annual routine. Like most teens, back-to-school shopping had become somewhat of a ritualized experience. With the summer quickly fading away, I was literally standing on edge waiting for my parents to make that glorious announcement.

Still nothing.

I remember mumbling to my mother, "I need some clothes."

Her response was always the same, "We're going."

My mind was riddled with confusion. Why were my parents procrastinating? What were they waiting for?

At first, I was simply concerned that I wouldn't be able to purchase all of what I thought I needed for school. Within a week of the first day, that concern elevated into fear. I was afraid that I'd have to return to school in the same old clothes and shoes from last year. When, I closed my eyes, I could imagine all the stares; everyone piercing at me through judgmental eyes.

I imagined that everyone would notice; that I'd stand out. They'd think we were poor. I'd be scarred forever. My entire high school experience would be ruined.

The clock continued to count down and, by the time we reached two or three days before the beginning of the school year, I was in a complete panic.

I can faintly recall the look on my mother's face. It was a look of disappointment, not in me, but in just how bothered I was by what was going on. She could see my distress and I think she was concerned by the fact that there was nothing she could do about it.

Then, the day I'd been dreading all summer finally arrived. It was the eve of the first day of school, and still, no school shopping had been done. I managed to squeeze a half-hearted promise out of my father who'd told me that he would give me the money that day. Once again, my hopes were dashed—it never happened.

Waking up on the first day of school, only a single thought traveled through my head. "I have no clothes."

There was no way that I could return to school on the first day with the same old clothes from last year. How was I supposed to start off my sophomore reign with the same old gear from my freshman days? It was in that moment that I decided to do the unthinkable. I staged a sit-in. Well, a *sleep*-in, if you will.

Here I am 30 years later, and I still can't believe it. Some may think refusing to go to school is a small infraction, but, in my house, insurrections were unheard of. We were raised on the, "do what you're told, when you're told" principle. There was no "board of directors" in our household. At 159th and Sawyer, my parents called the shots. There was no democracy—a love-filled dictatorship, at best—but there was never any resistance from the ranks of children. For me to muster up the courage to take that self-righteous stand was like David standing up to slay Goliath. Caught in the moment, I did what I felt was right, but I still had no idea of how that day would play out.

Defiantly glued to my bed, I listened as my father yelled down the stairs.

"Time to get up!" That was my cue.

Instead of obliging, I yelled back up, "I don't have any clothes!"

The admission sent tears streaming down my face. I was breaking down by the minute.

I didn't know what to expect; part of me was waiting to be dragged out the front door by my ankles. But, to my absolute amazement, my parents didn't say a thing. In fact, I missed the first three days of my sophomore year without objection.

By the fourth day of my protest, my parents had enough. That morning, I heard my father walk to the top of the basement stairs. He called my name. Prying myself out of the bed, I walked to the bottom of the stairs and looked up at him. A few moments passed, and all I could see was the stern look written all over his face. Finally, he broke the silence.

"Here you go, boy," he said. Then, a crisp fifty-dollar bill slowly floated down the stairwell. I watched as it danced in the air, veering to the left, bouncing off a wall, then landing at my feet. "Go and get you some clothes."

With his permission, I gathered myself as quickly as I could. Scurrying to the bus stop, all it would take was a 15-minute ride to get me to River Oaks mall. My destination was Marshall's department store, I was sure they had all I needed.

Just as I suspected, I was able to stretch that fifty-dollar bill to the max. I purchased three pairs of pants, three shirts, and a pair of shoes. In full on desperation mode, I stopped to place an extra pair of pants in my bag on the way out the door. That's a nice way of saying I stole a pair of pants.

My mission was accomplished. With about two or three "good" pairs of pants left over from last year, I knew that haul would be enough to carry me through. And, with no need to continue my protest, I made it to the fifth day of school.

That was yet another transformative moment in my life. You see, the moral of this story isn't standing your ground until you get what you want. The real jewel didn't hit me until long after.

Today, I probably have a ridiculous number of pants—approximately one hundred pairs; but to borrow my wife's defense, I live in a four-season city—yet, strangely now, I look forward to wearing the same pair of pants twice in a row. It's a small form of liberation for me now. On those "lazy" days, I get to be free. I use it as a small form of protest against the confines of society's scrutiny, or what I have created it to be. Those days give me one less thing to worry about; one less problem to solve. I'm also reminded of "how far I've travelled."

I'm transported back to sophomore year in those moments in other ways. I think of how selfish I was; how blinded I'd been by superficial wants and needs. After all, my parents sacrificed for me on a daily basis; it wasn't until I was a full-grown adult that I could even begin to process their commitment, to properly interpret their expressions on that fateful day. The blankness in their stares was riddled with pain. I don't think I'll ever escape the guilt of that memory.

What was cause for a "sit-in" in 1985, is now cause for a consciousness of gratitude for the sacrifices of my parents. Me imagining them bearing the burden of providing food, water, shelter, clothing, and occasional splurges for entertainment for five children—it's impressive by any standard.

Although things didn't exactly "click" until later in my adult years, that period in my life significantly shaped my reality. The summer of '85 was the last time my parents ever had to purchase clothes for me.

From that moment forward, I assumed the responsibility of making sure that I had clothes for school or for any other reason a teenage boy may have wanted to get dressed up. Aside from the occasional pair of shoes, I never had the nerve to bother them for any sort of extensive shopping.

Going forward, it became my mission to never be in that position again.

I became more resourceful than ever. By the time winter hit, while others may have seen snowfall as a free day off, I saw it as opportunity.

The math seemed straight forward enough to me: If I were hired to shovel the snow in driveways at $15 each, all it'd take was two customers for me to pocket $30. With thirty dollars, I could buy myself another pair of pants and a shirt to match... and have money to spare.

When spring and summer came back around, I spent my sunny Saturday afternoons on the prowl. Borrowing the lawnmower for a few hours, I'd knock on 20 or so doors. If I could get three houses to say "yes," at $10-15 dollars per yard, that was a great day for a young entrepreneur.

Two more shirts in my wardrobe, and a couple more dollars in my pocket.

Wanting and the Necessity to be Somewhat Self-reliant were the Drivers of my Pathway to Entrepreneurship.

Again, not knowing it at the time, the foundation was being laid for my entry into the world of entrepreneurship.

What's funny is, by my senior year I didn't even care about what I wore to school anymore. I distinctly remember my first day, I walked in the door wearing sweatpants and a t-shirt. I didn't care about what anyone thought. It's amazing how things can change so drastically in such a short amount of time.

What I've come to realize is, oftentimes, our relationship to things—clothes, cars, jewelry, etc.—is likely rooted in some sort of insecurity, frequently connected to fundamentally arbitrary variables such as race, economic status, and gender. Despite what I thought, I wasn't really concerned about the clothes.

I was worried about my peers thinking I was poor. I didn't want anybody looking at me like I couldn't afford the latest and greatest that everybody else wore. I didn't want to be defined by what I had on. I didn't want to be viewed as different, odd, or an outsider.

I wanted the comfort of "fitting in". I needed those clothes as a security blanket, one that guaranteed my place inside society's box.

There's an old adage that goes, "poor people remain poor by trying to appear rich; and rich people remain rich by living and looking relatively poor".

I was playing the game as if I were a poor man; wanting to appear as if I had more. Of course, this is a heavy burden for a fifteen-year-old. To be asked to not succumb to peer pressure. To adopt values that many people twice his age are unable to maintain. Yet, they are asked to be and do so much more in other ways.

It took some undoing, but that experience was a first step toward a journey of reconditioning. I had to divorce myself from a pattern of thinking influenced by my concern of what others' perception of me may be.

And, if you are thinking this is confined to a fifteen-year-old, I contend you are mistaken. Look no further than in the pews of churches across the country. Pastor Prada and Deacon Designer spreading the Gospel to hundreds of members sporting new clothes from head to toe, while drowning in debt, praying to God to save them from the fifteen-year-old who is inside of them making financial decisions. Many will literally spearhead a "sit-in" on Sunday morning, the same as me in 1985, if they "feel" they do not have adequate clothes to wear to take in the word of God himself. I'm saying if God himself were going to be delivering the message, they may not show if their "outfit" was not to their standard. Ok, you should know by now, I can be a bit over the top!

Every year, millions of people send themselves spiraling into debt because they want to "keep up with the Joneses," so to speak. This vicious cycle isn't exclusive to society's economically lower or middle class. Sitting at the top of the totem pole, you'll find Vice Presidents of banks and major corporations that spend their days having subconscious tantrums with the poor little boys and girls they've buried within. They max out their corporate spending accounts and treat themselves to lavish sprees at Macy's because they've trained themselves to believe that's what they're "supposed" to do. Social media keeps us enthralled by the lifestyle of the rich and famous, and people become fixated on the need to satisfy the innate desire to be a part of the "haves" rather than the "have nots".

To be clear, I'm not saying we should all walk around in shags and rags. I'm a firm believer that bad fashion is one of the cardinal sins (it's a joke…kinda), but that doesn't take away from the fact that the culture of consumption is killing many of us, and I mean that in both the literal and figurative sense.

Many in America are drowning in debt to support our consumption addiction.

As a consequence, CNN Money reported in 2017 nearly six in 10 Americans "don't have enough savings to cover a $500 or $1,000 unplanned expense," according to a Bankrate report.

Also, a November 2018 article in Smart Asset titled "Where Is the Average Savings Account Balance?", using data from the Federal Reserve Survey of Consumer Finances, reported the average American household as having a median savings of $5,200. By race, White Non-Hispanic's had a median savings of $7,140, Hispanics $1,500, and Blacks $1,000.

I feel somewhat fortunate in being able to draw one of many parallels of moments in my life that went toward shaping the less productive part of my relationship with money and spending. We've all had similar experiences, they just may not have ended up with a silent protest and a stolen pair of jeans just to get your point across. (Hey— don't judge me. Desperate times call for desperate measures!) That experience moved me to vow that I would never allow myself to be in the position to "want" for anything. It marked the beginning of my lifelong pledge to be reasonably self-sufficient and never burden my parents with another petty tantrum.

No less, if you think long enough, I'm sure you'll be able to pinpoint at least one time when everything you thought about work and money was changed forever. I want you to trace your memory until you can pinpoint your moment, then decide how you plan to release yourself. We can find ourselves stuck in cycles, but those barriers can be broken. No matter how long you've held on to those quintessential beliefs, you can undo what's been done.

Learning to define yourself on your own terms would be step one. Developing an unwavering opinion of self is the key to breaking away from the society's materialistic definition. If all 100 pairs of my pants vanished tomorrow, it wouldn't put a dent in the man I am. I've worked hard to define myself outside of tangible possessions.

Today I ask you to define yourself, for yourself—on your own terms. Find the strength to start making small adjustments in your thinking, to start redefining your being.

Chapter 4

Sometimes When You Are Losing, You Are Winning. and Sometimes When You Are Winning, You Are Losing.

It wasn't enough I was still adjusting from moving from Chicago's southside a few days shy of my fifth birthday. I left that all-black concrete oasis to live in white suburbia with backyard swimming pools and plum and pear trees. I'm still confused as to the use of rhubarb. I just know we'd pull up big stalks of it and chew on it for its bitter juice.

I enrolled in Markham Park Elementary School with my two other siblings. My brother was a few grades above me; my sister one grade ahead of him. I was maybe one of seven black kids in a class of 25 or so. I had never interacted with non-black folk in such close quarters. The difference of being black was always present.

I was a silent competitor at the outset. Oh, so you want me to color. No problem, I can color better than everyone in the classroom. Write the alphabet in cursive? No problem, my handwriting will be better than everyone in the class; even the girls. Oh, stop it; we all know the girls had better penmanship than boys.

It took a year before I felt really noticed. It was first for my "spirited" behavior. I was always an aggressive and energetic kid. Then my second-grade teacher, Ms. Doris, seemed to take notice. I would consistently be one of the faster and more accurate students on our arithmetic and time table drills.

I remember relishing the opportunity to race the clock and be called out as one of the top finishers. There were pink and blue test sheets. The equation was written above an opening on the test sheet. We had to place the test grid on a sheet of paper and write our answer on the paper inside the cut out box.

"Ok. Please remove everything from your desk. Make certain you have a sharpened pencil and nothing else. Do not turn the test over until I say go. You have two minutes to complete as many as you can. There are 82 questions on each test. If you look at the person's test next to you, don't bother. They have different questions than you. Now, GO!"

My nemesis and first-grade best friend and I would frantically begin. We competed in almost everything. Math tests, off the wall, dodge ball, the high jump. You name it, and it became competition for us. To preserve his identity, I'll call him Smooth. He was always really laid back. He showed as much or more promise as I early on. I always tried to make certain to stay ahead of him.

As a result of my natural inclination to do well in math, in particular, I quickly was accepted as one of the smart kids. But what was unusual about me was that I was also considered one of the "bad" kids. Although I was a good student, my behavior overshadowed my academic aptitude. To my elementary school teachers' credit, they did their best to sway my energy more toward academics than mischief and dodge ball.

I recall being grouped with the five or six "brainiacs" (as we called them) in elementary school to assist other students or work on projects. When it first happened, I thought it was some type of experiment I was unknowingly a part of. I mean, these kids weren't the friends I hung out with. They didn't play dodge ball during gym or "off the wall" before school. Off the wall is a game requiring a tennis ball and a nice flat wall high enough to slam the ball against. The objective is to catch the ball before it hits the ground. If you caught the ball before it hit the ground, you were allowed to be the thrower.

Also, these weren't the kids we played strike him out (or just strike out) with after school or basketball and football on the weekend. And, they most certainly weren't amongst the group who took turns as spectator and gladiator in after school scuffles.

So, why was I called in the hallway to work with them. You must understand this was very alarming to me.

In middle school, the science teacher, whom we tortured by having all-out spitball wars, saw enough in me to do the same. He had a very raspy and deep voice. He always sounded like he needed to swallow. "Ernest. Come here. You and David and Tracy and [a few names I can't recall] are going to work on a project in the library." Again, I'm like, "why me? Are they setting me up for something?" I knew the others in the group were well-behaved and above average performing students. It took me a week or so before I stopped waiting to be pulled from the group, imagining the conversation: "Ernest, why are you with this group? You shouldn't be here."

In any event, despite my mischievous ways and penchant for finding myself in after school brawls, I was an A and B student throughout elementary and middle school. I was robbed of honor roll by my perennial C's in Music and Gym: grades more reflective of my behavior and not my performance.

Years later I realized the significant impact of my formative education and experience. I was the smart black kid who was earmarked as salvageable, by some, and promising, by fewer. Many of my classmates were not as fortunate as I. In these early years, I developed a confidence that many of my peers lacked. Confidence that I could compete, that I was as smart as any other kid in my class, and that others are no smarter than I am and just as lost in many instances too.

I had the benefit of many caring but stern teachers.

They say you don't appreciate what you have until it's gone. There were no truer words spoken, as I learned upon entering high school.

The pats on the back were gone. The teacher telling me how smart I am was gone. It's like now I was treated more as a problem. Again, I was no angel. However,…

It is at this critical stage many young African American boys in particular are lost. We are informed by our environment, media, and in my case educational institutions, that we are a problem.

Many give up hope in the moment and resign to the subculture of gangs, drugs, and violence where they are accepted and celebrated.

It is the modern-day Middle Passage.

In 1984 I was being bused for the first time to school.

The high school I attended in the mid-eighties was relatively recently integrated with black kids like me: the ones bused in from the neighboring suburbs. Tinley Park High School was located in a community ninety-nine percent Caucasian. Ten percent of the high school population was bused in from my neighborhood and a few others. It wasn't uncommon to be called a Nigger while playing a competitive game of basketball. Me being me, I would respond, "Cracker." And we'd face up to establish our common commitment to our pride, before being separated in most instances.

I'm not certain to what extent this new culture contributed to a noticeable decline in my performance. In fairness, the relative lack of accountability and freedom in high school as compared to middle school certainly had something to do with it. And my parents never were involved on a day-to-day basis with my education. My mother attended all of the parent-teacher conferences and made certain to check my report card. But there was never much more than that. I think she was accustomed to me always making the grade and my own way.

In high school however my prospects for the future started to become somewhat uncertain. My prognosis would sound very different depending on who you asked. I'm sure my father would have said, "the boy is going to be whatever he wants to be...and rich," with his signature smirk and accompanying laugh. As to say, "what a silly question." My mother may have said, "I don't know about that boy." Lol. I know for certain what the Dean of my high school would have said. Nothing good for sure. Let's just call my high school Dean Mr. D. Mr. D seemed to be an all-American blonde-haired blue-eyed white man. His son was an All-Conference point guard at a competing high school. He was always immaculately dressed and in seemingly great shape. I don't think Mr. D disliked me or anyone who looked like me. I just think he didn't understand us, like many of the staff.

Just the same as it was my first experience with white people; it too was their relatively first experience with me. So much of what is easily assigned as racism is a misunderstanding and discomfort between two people, from seemingly two different worlds, thrust together.

I was far from a poster child in high school. I was a consistent resident of in-school suspension and after-school detention. I was the kid who liked to chat it up, pass notes, and test the boundaries of the teachers' patience with my nagging behavior. I was a nuisance, at best. By today's standard of a troubled student, I'd be a poster child. There was no fighting or cursing at the teacher. Certainly, there was no physical challenges to the teacher. I have to admit, I was irritating.

Despite my propensity as a "troubled" student, I was relatively conscious of the necessity to at least earn passing grades in my classes, albeit the hard way. Now remember, I always made the grade in elementary and middle school. Well, I learned quickly in high school my reputation had not preceded me. My nightmare started first semester, first year, in English 101. The teacher was an African American woman who seemed to have a perpetual snarl. At least with me and my crew. I took my usual cocky attitude into her classroom. I'll pay attention when I decide to pay attention. I'll hurry the completion of my homework ten minutes before you ask it to be passed to the front of the classroom. And I'll study for the exam on the bus heading to school on the scheduled day of the test.

I guess you can figure where I'm headed? The UNTHINKABLE!!! She FAILED ME! The ice cream man was gone, McDonald's was closing its doors, dodge ball was being banned, and Michael Jordan was leaving the Chicago Bulls. I mean that's what it felt like when I saw my report card with that Big Ugly F. I had worked my plan flawlessly. First and second grading period I had earned a D. She "gave" me an F on the final and an F in the class. That meant I had to do it all over again. I had wasted an entire semester enduring English and her. Ok, I'm over it. Moving on.

Sometimes when you think you are losing, you are winning. Sometimes, when you think you are winning, you are losing.

Anyhow, this experience taught me a valuable lesson:

The world is not going to lay down for me, no matter how smart I thought I was; I had to put in work.

From that day forward I was on a mission to "defeat high school!"

Here's my plan.

1. I will never fail another class and waste my time.
2. I will make certain to earn at least a C first marking period. At least a D second marking period. With a C and D, even if I failed the finals, my final grade would be no less than a passing D.
3. I will take six classes each semester rather than five. If I must be in school, I might as well be earning credits.

I executed my plan to perfection. I became a smart C minus student. Just like I had planned. I gave minimal effort, and I received minimal reward in return. Again, in hindsight, I view high school as the Middle Passage for many African American men in particular, which seems to be largely supported by the historically disparate high school dropout rates. Prior to the year 2000, African American men between the ages of 16–24 were almost twice as likely to drop out of high school than our white counterparts. These statistics were reported by the National Center for Education Statistics, a federal agency within the United States Department of Education. They are mandated to collect, collate, analyze, and report complete statistics on the condition of American education. Fortunately, since 2000, the gap between has essentially dissipated.

Although the issue of race is heavily implicated in my experience, the story is not so different for black boys in all-black school districts all over the country. What's strange is what almost happened to me (being lost in the shuffle) in 1984 is still happening more than thirty years later.

I was one of the lucky ones. I could have just as easily been lost in the Middle Passage too. I had a few definite and significant advantages. I was raised in a two-parent household for one. And I was indoctrinated early on with the belief I was smart and somewhat special. With all of my advantages, I somehow was reduced to a C minus student. I could have easily have been a B plus and honor roll student. Remember, I was a C minus student throughout high school. In fact, I recall having almost all Ds on my report card one marking period. After insulating myself from failure by attaining a B or C in every class the first marking period, I would simply take the rest of the semester off. Fine, give me a D for the second grading period. Fine, I'm not studying for finals. And, voilà, Ds across the board.

Nevertheless, my master plan was still in effect. I never failed another class in high school. I was simply failing myself. Many of us are operating in life as I did in high school. We are engaged in a game to survive various aspects of our life. Settling on the D.

We've sold ourselves on the story that "getting by" is good enough. That having just enough money to meet our monthly obligations is good enough. That having an ok relationship is not that bad. We've settled into our comfortable world of underachievement and mediocrity, at best. In this world, studying is not required. Preparation is not required.

Well, remember my plan? Part of my plan was to maximize my time so I could finish high school as soon as possible. Well, I may have sold out on being a good student, but I certainly never lost focus on surviving high school.

While my peers were taking five classes per semester, I was taking six. I even enrolled myself in summer school to make up the lost time after failing English 101, with that dreadful woman (lol).

As Fate would have it, in the beginning of my final semester of high school in spring of 1987, I had only one mandatory subject to graduate: ENGLISH. Here we go again, the only class I ever failed in my life was standing in my way of flawlessly (in my warped way of thinking) executing my plan.

I was on pace to graduate early from high school despite being a C minus student.

For the first time in my high school career, I took my book home on a regular basis. I studied days in advance for quizzes and exams. I scored my very first A in high school the first semester grading period. I followed it up with an A the second marking period and received a final grade of an A for the class.

I remember realizing I was about to actually earn an A in a class.

My elementary school nemesis and early best friend, Mr. Smooth, was in my class. While I had devolved into an uninspired student, he had one-upped me to become a drug dealer. Given his new found stature, he had resigned to copy my homework and cheat off my paper during test time. Of course, like me, he too had no intention on pursuing education after high school. He was already in the midst of a successful career path as a drug dealer. He would

37

come to school in silk shirts and gold jewelry. He'd show me wads of money and smile at his growing prominence. Despite being from a seemingly stable two-parent working class household, he was lost in the Middle Passage.

Now the moment of truth was upon us. I had aced English and gathered 30.25 credits in three-and-one-half years. What's odd is I never shared my plan with anyone other than one or two of my friends. My parents were unaware; the teachers were unaware; and the Dean, Mr. D, was certainly unaware.

In order to graduate early, I had to have the Dean sign off, or certify, I had met the high school credit requirement and submit the documentation to the proper department at the School District.

I remember the day like it was yesterday. I strolled into the Principal's office and took a seat. This time I was not summoned there by the Dean for admonishment or pushed out by a disgruntled teacher for some smart retort to a question. This time I was there on my own terms. It was payback time. I was about to shake up the world, much the same way my hero Muhammad Ali did in Zaire against George Foreman in 1974 in the "Rumble in the Jungle."

Mr. D was in his office. He looked around the corner and said, "Ernest, what are you doing here?" I said, "I'm here to have you sign off on my paper to graduate." He said, "to graduate?" in a very confused tone. I said back, "I'm graduating early." He stood up and walked out. He looked at me and said, "Are you graduating?" He was asking if I was graduating at all. He thought I was one of the many black kids that would be lost in the Middle Passage. I said again, "I'm graduating early." He said, "let me see that paper." On the paper was listed my final semester classes, the teachers' names, and the grades in each class. Peculiarly pronounced, and what I was most proud of, was my A in English. In order to include the credits from the final semester the teachers had to sign off on my final grade in their class. Mr. D went into his office. He rumbled through some papers. He asked the secretary to retrieve some papers. After a short while, he emerged from his office, shook my hand, looked at me with absolute disbelief, and said, "good luck."

There is latent genius in students who have been stripped of their passion to be great. The predators of these young men and others assume many forms. They occupy places of esteem in politics. They unevenly dispense justice in robes, under the guise of impartiality as Judges. In their most sinister form they will subconsciously blunt your passion to align with their lowered expectations of themselves, in their exalted role as friend and family. This is not a burden of few to overcome, this is a burden of many.

The blessing is that none of these forces are powerful enough to deny your will, if you will! And, if you work!

Chapter 5

The Military: The Best and Worse Experience of My Life

June 1987 marked the beginning of my final semester of high school. That final semester quickly proved to be my final test in surviving the trials of the public school system. All I needed to do was make it through a few more months. It was going to go by quickly, at least that's what I thought.

As motivation, I carried around what I titled my "master plan" in my front right pocket. Handwritten on a half-sized sheet of ruled paper, my "master plan" was a list of four major milestones I set out to conquer. I knew I had to do four things in order for my life to feel complete:

#1 – Graduate High School Early

#2 – Enlist in the Military

#3 – Buy a Car

#4 – Buy a Motorcycle

That was it. Were you expecting something more elaborate? Well, despite its lack of sophistication, these four things became the driving force behind my leap into "adulting." Motivated by the self-described mastery of my plan, I read—and reread—that list several times each day. I shared its existence with only a couple of friends; passing them in the hallway with a smile, I'd touch the outside of my pocket and say something like, "Working that master plan!" I didn't realize it at the time, I was speaking my success into existence...

Or maybe I was creating accountability for myself by sharing my goals with others. Either way, it's a practice that I still use to this day.

Prior to high school graduation, I began the process of enlisting in the military. I was 17 years of age and needed my parents' consent to enlist. They didn't hesitate to oblige. I don't care to speculate over why. I like to imagine they simply loved me dearly and trusted my judgement. We'll just assume that it had nothing to do with all those sleepless nights I caused while "coming into my own." Whatever the reason, having their signatures on the dotted line turned into a decision that forever changed my life.

I can remember when I first broke the news. We were passing each other in the kitchen, and I think I mumbled something like, "I need you all to sign off on papers so I can go into the military." No warming them up, I got straight to the point. It was probably the best my 17-year-old mind could muster. The best my mother could do was repeat the last two words of my statement. "The military." Her voice was steady, but it was clear that I caught her off guard. My father's response was along the lines of, "Alright, hope you're ready." And that was that.

No more than two weeks after having that impromptu "talk" with my parents, my recruiter, Sergeant Tito, was in that very same kitchen, sitting at the table with my family. We went over my enlistment papers, got everything signed, and, just a few weeks later, I was in downtown Chicago taking the Armed Services Vocational Battery (ASVAB) test. This test determines which jobs you'll be qualified to have in the military; higher scores meant more career options.

Most were concerned with having options, but my approach was much different. I was only interested in getting one of the highest scores—for me, it was just a competition.

It seemed as if my teenage mind was on to something. Prior to taking that test, I didn't know it, but there was much more at stake than just obtaining the opportunity to have specialty choices in my military role. The ASVAB also played a major part in determining how many years I had to enlist once I was enrolled. Back then, most people believed that the military required a minimum of four years of duty. Well, I shocked everyone (again) when I confessed that my "master plan" had a side note beside that "enlist in the military goal"—I only planned to serve for two years. That was it! I refused to sign up for any longer than that. Let's just say that Sergeant Tito wasn't too thrilled over the news. In fact, he didn't think a two-year enlistment was even possible. That is, until I aced the ASVAB and proved that nothing was impossible, if you put your mind to it.

Given my two-year enlistment offer, I had few specialty options to choose from. I ultimately signed on as a 62 Bravo, Heavy Construction Equipment Repairer. Yeah, you read it correctly! Heavy Construction Equipment Repairer. Just four months after beginning the last semester of my senior year, my 17-year-old self was well on his way to crossing off the first two objectives of my "master plan." I signed off and was set to go as of October 1987.

It had to be sometime during the next month when my Aunt Nita came to visit us from St. Louis. My mother's side of the family would oftentimes visit for Thanksgiving; I'm assuming that's why she was in town. Standing in the very same kitchen where I broke the news to my parents, she posed the question most everyone wanted to know.

"Why are you going to the military, nephew?" Her words echoed in the air, but my motives were clear.

"I want to buy a car and a motorcycle—and I want to save some money," I proudly confessed.

She paused. I watched her eyes as she searched her mind for the right words. "You know they don't pay that much money in the military, right?" She tried to let me down as gently as she could.

"I know, but I can do it." I sensed her caution, but I was so self-assured. There was nothing anyone could do or say to shake me up.

I will never forget that exchange, not because of what she said but because it made me even more determined to accomplish my goals.

"They must not think I can do it"—the revelation bounced around in my head. Regardless of who did or did not believe in the likelihood of my success, I was fixated on accomplishing every single goal on my list.

The wealthiest of men are not necessarily the ones who make the most money; the wealthiest of men are those who have managed to keep the most money.

There was no context for me to assume such a grandiose personal challenge. At the ripe age of 17, my "budgeting skills" left a lot to the imagination. Still, I felt like I was doing what was best for my future. Weighing my options, it was clear to me that two years in the military was the easiest way for me to secure the path I wanted to carve out for myself. Considering what life was like in Chicago in the 80s, there was no place I'd rather be than away in the military. I prepared for my send-off with my mind made up, armed with nothing more than the ignorant bliss of a teenage boy—and the drive to follow through on my word.

January 16, 1988: I checked off the #1 goal on my master plan. My life seemed to graduate, both literally and figuratively, when I *finally* completed my last semester of high school. On February 10th, not even a month later, Private Fenton was officially being shipped off to Basic Training in Ft. Leonard Wood, Missouri.

Just like that, #2 was checked off the list too!

Then, reality swept in and hit me like a bag of bricks.

To put it plainly, Ft. Leonard Wood was anything but a dream station. In fact, it was nicknamed Ft. Misery—a term I'd learn to understand sooner rather than later. Located in the middle of a non-descript town with little to do on base, Ft. Leonard Wood left a lot to the imagination. The winters were too cold, and summers were excruciatingly hot. There wasn't much around in terms of entertainment or distractions. Luckily, it was only meant to be my home for a relatively short time. After eight weeks of basic training and nine weeks of Advanced Individual Training (AIT), I could make my escape. In the meantime, it was onward with the mission at hand.

As a part of our orientation, we were advised to set up a bank account. To be honest, it was the first time in my life that the idea ever crossed my mind. Even with my brilliantly-laid 4-step master plan, I was nothing like that wiz kid from IKEA that I would come to meet more than two decades later. As I mentioned, I was new to the whole "adulting" thing. On advisement, I went ahead and opened the account so my monthly pay could be sent via direct deposit. Back then, the concept was new and quite intriguing to me. At the end of the month, someone was going to be dropping a sum of money into my account. The way they explained it, I'd just wake up one day, check my balance, and the money would be there—waiting. Say no more. I'm all in!

I opened my first account at a local bank that wasn't too far from my parents' home. My mother drove me to the branch, and I asked if she wanted to be a joint holder on my new savings account, in case I needed money in an emergency; *only* for emergencies. Other than that, my strategy was to save as much as I could over the next two years. As fate would have it, that mission would prove to be more challenging than most were willing to accept but, even as a teenager, I never gave myself any other option. With the savings account at a small bank, I knew I wouldn't have direct access to my money, which meant it wouldn't be easy for me to be tempted by accessibility. Like many of my most brilliant ideas, my plan was simple. Whatever money that went to that account was off limits.

I made a commitment to let the money pile up for two years. No checking accounts linked to the savings—that would've gone against my limited access plan. I kept things as basic as my circumstances would allow. Even with limited banking experience, I realized that the savings account was the best route for me. Not only would my money accrue interest as it piled up over the next two years, savings accounts require time and effort to retrieve your money. Remember, this was the late 80s. We didn't have luxuries like Apple Pay and online banking. There weren't any apps to help you transfer funds from account to account. Direct Deposit was still a new phenomenon to some. With the way my account was set up, if I wanted to get my money out of the bank, I had to go through my mother.

My father taught me how to hustle for money; my mother taught me how to keep it.

Thinking back, I don't think I really appreciated all that went into making that decision. Being so young but having the discipline to set myself up for success, never giving failure an option; these qualities helped carry me through many trials. I didn't come to realize how precious it was for me to have someone whom I could trust with my life savings until many years later. It never occurred to me that my mother could have withdrawn my money at any time. I just knew I needed a lifeline while I was away, and, without a second thought, she seemed like the best person to entrust with that responsibility.

After four long weeks of crawling, push-ups, cleaning toilets, humiliation, starvation, sleepless nights, and pulling guard duty at 2 A.M., I was rewarded a check for approximately $550. Then, it all made sense. Through all the questions and concerned looks I got from family and friends, through battling the doubt and anxiety they were unintentionally trying to deposit into my spirit, when I finally received that first check, everything came together for me. *That* was why I enlisted.

I know you may see the figure and laugh now, but, back then, 550 bucks was a nice little payday—especially for an ambitious teen with no bills or responsibilities. As a matter of fact, it was more money than I'd ever received at once. Sure, there were plenty of people in my platoon that weren't impressed, but I was just fine with the salary. Hell, after a month of grueling military labor, I was finally getting paid! I didn't have any complaints.

Three hundred and fifty dollars were deposited into my account. I kept a crisp one-hundred-dollar bill in my right pocket. That day, I made a vow. From then on, I would always keep $100 in my pocket as sort of a symbolic gesture. It was a reminder of my mission. It kept me focused. The remaining one hundred dollars was for toiletries, shoe polish, and contraband (that's what we call cookies, Snickers, smokes for some, and other junk food).

The next month, four hundred and fifty dollars were deposited. Now, I had $800 in the bank. Again, more money than I ever managed in a single sitting. I set my direct deposit at four hundred dollars per month thereafter.

By month three, I knew I had $1,200 in the bank. Month four left me with $1,600. By the fifth month, I reached the $2,000 milestone. Next, I'd reach $3,000, and so on. To me, savings became somewhat of a game. A game of discipline. A game of "surviving" on $150 per month. As an 18-year-old with zero adult oversight in my personal affairs, this was an especially daunting task. Sure, I wanted to visit the malls and shop like my peers. And I could have done it, if I wanted to, but I trained my mind to look beyond those temporary distractions. I had a long-term goal in mind, and I knew I had to stick to my monthly budget. More important than my budget, I remembered *what* I was playing for. Whenever I was faced with temptation, I stopped and thought about the goals I had set for myself while still in high school. After having a small taste of success while turning the first half of my goals into a two-for-one victory, I must admit, I wanted that feeling again. What seemed like an unnecessary sacrifice to some was really just a necessary step on my quest for self-validation.

Let's be clear, I'm the guy who lives by the philosophy that "bad fashion is a sin." I'd go as far as to say I am a fashion "junkie." To make matters worse, I was transferred from Ft. Misery to my permanent duty station in Fulda, West Germany in July 1988. Other than the culture shock and the Cold War, I had to contend with the temptation of European fashion. The Italian shoes. The cashmere jackets. The raw regal appeal. I couldn't get enough of it.

Back home, I never saw old men as "cool." If I closed my eyes to picture an old man, I saw dirty jeans and a faded t-shirt with a stretched-out collar, maybe even a pair of overalls or something. Whatever I was accustomed to in the US was nothing like what I saw in Europe. Those old men had on loafers, nice colored cords, luxe cashmere sweaters with long wool overcoats, and matching scarves. Of course, you can't forget the fitted gloves that masterfully completed the look.

Each month, I'd take my meager budget to the local shops. The first time I went, I was able to snag a cashmere jacket. By the next month, I was the owner of a nice pair of Italian shoes. Since hindsight is 20/20, now I see how the discipline and patience I was forced to learn from middle school to high school served me pretty well in the military. There I was, in an entirely different stage of my life, trying to figure out how to buy clothes all over again. Instead, this time around, the experience was much different. I had access to more money than I ever had as a teen, but, while making the first steps into manhood, I'd learned the power of delayed gratification. The understanding I gathered after my makeshift high school sit-in helped me learn to trust the process and appreciate small victories. I may not have gone on elaborate shopping sprees, but I learned to balance my wants and needs. Even if I managed to buy a new pair of socks, that was something worth celebrating. It was one more pair of socks than I had the last month; one more thing that I bought for myself within my budget.

When we're children, we can think of our parents like alien creatures sent to Earth on a mission to make our lives as miserable as they possibly can. By the time I made it to the military, I learned how to appreciate the lessons I learned from the past. Sticking to that budget gave me an inkling of the value that comes when you don't get everything handed to you by your parents. While I was training myself to live on my newly established budget, it became easier for me to accept the fact that I couldn't have everything I wanted right away. I understood that, sometimes, there was a process we had to follow to get those "wants"; sometimes we had to work really hard to earn life's luxuries.

After six months of military service, Privates were automatically promoted to Enlisted 2, or Private Second Class. With that promotion, I received a $100 increase to my monthly salary. Because of that, I eventually earned a whopping $650 per month. Let's see how well you know me by now—what do you think was my next move?

I'll tell you this, soldiers are notoriously bad about saving money. Most of my friends were broke the first week after payday. To even suggest that they were saving anything was laughable. The vast majority of young enlisted men followed the same narrative. I, on the other hand, was notorious for squeezing juice from a five-dollar bill.

Friday night, you'd find me walking almost two miles to get to the local club hangout where most soldiers frequented. When the club closed at 1 AM, I'd walk back to the barracks. The cab ride was $3 or $4. I wasn't about to pay that!

When I was in the club, I'd see everyone else ordering drinks back to back (the legal drinking age in Germany was sixteen). I'd walk right up to the bartender and say, "I'll have a water, thank you." If I felt like splurging, I may have coughed up the $1 for a soft drink, but that was it. I wasn't spending a penny more. It wasn't in my budget.

This ideology followed me wherever I went. I don't think you can imagine just how happy I was to discover one of my age-old favorites while I was deployed. McDonald's! Yes, there was a European McDonald's, and, although it was a lot different than the magical land I grew to love as a child, my visits still became one of the highlights of my week. It took a little time for me to adjust to the fact that the menu had been modified to appeal to European pallets. Even still, I made the best of it. When in Rome, you do as the Romans, right? Well, in this case, I guess it should be, "when in Germany…"

Nevertheless, I found myself standing at the counter once again. As a man with a plan, actively saving most of his salary and busting his butt to earn every cent, I was in a much different space from where I was when I made that pivotal trip with my childhood friend. My buddies, on the other hand, obviously took a page from his book. They'd stand at the counter and say, "I'll have a Big Mac, large fry, and large shake." After paying for their feast, they'd step aside for me, and I'd clear my throat to recite, "Uh, I'll have two cheeseburgers, a small fry, and a cup of water." If I was really splurging, I'd add a sundae. But the real eye-opener to this story is how ironic life can be.

In November 1989, a few months short of my discharge date, the Berlin Wall fell. East Germans rushed across the border in the thousands. I posted up with other soldiers and greeted them; "where?," do you ask? At McDonald's of course! I swear McDonald's owes me money for this. Lol. Anyhow, I wasn't pinching my "dollars" too much that evening. I spent all of the deutsche marks in my pocket purchasing hamburgers and french fries for East Germans excited to experience the Golden Arches for the first time. I still have a piece of the stone collected that evening from the collapse of the Wall at my mother's home.

There I was, yet again, learning a life lesson at McDonald's. *The irony of freedom not being free. Opportunity is an asset that should be cherished. And, your "enemy" is just as afraid of you as you are of them.* This time, I had to enlist in the military and cross an entire ocean to learn that lesson in a foreign land, but it was a *valuable* lesson—one I'm passing on to you today.

Saving was a priority, one that could not be super-seded by superficiality. I didn't care about what "everybody else was doing." If I let myself get wrapped up in following the crowd, I would've been just as broke as everyone else.

Some may think I was being ridiculous. They may believe I should've given in at some point to "live a little." Being deployed in Germany was a unique experience. I'm sure there are people who think I missed out on an opportunity to enjoy myself without limits, to reap the benefits of being a military man in a foreign land. Well, if you are one of those people, you may want to skip this paragraph. When that $100 bonus kicked in, I didn't use it to feed my fashion addiction. I didn't find it a good enough excuse to start taking the cab to the club and throw back a few shots at the bar. Instead, I doubled down on my "crazy" and increased my direct deposit to $500 per month.

Now, I can look back at my unwavering commitment and laugh, but, back then, I was on a highway-to-hell mission. My friends would joke about it all the time, throwing shots at me about my frugal nature.

"Fenton is tough on a dollar."

"Fenton will only order a cup of water."

You're darn right. It seemed like everybody in the military had a back story, and, with my mission in mind, stretching my pennies as far as I could became mine. And, for the next 16 months, that was my life.

Desire requires sacrifice. That's the part of the equation that so many people miss. In the moment, it can feel like you're risking too much. It can feel as if you're making a disproportionate investment of time, energy, and resources, but that's just what it takes. As a practicing attorney who's counseled at least 5,000 clients on financial matters, I can confidently say that I've discovered a common denominator over the years. In short, most people are unwilling to make the sacrifices they need to make to have the life they wish to live.

It's not hard to save, most just don't know how to make saving a priority; far too many people think it's optional, like it's some kind of grown-up bonus that makes you a better adult. I've met people who refused to give up a $250 cable bill so they could comfortably afford their mortgage. It has always amazed me to see how many people will literally be months away from losing their home to foreclosure but will go out in the midst of that storm and purchase a $20,000 car. Rather than make the roof over their heads a priority, they'd prefer to sign on the dotted line for a 18% interest rate that's going to place them in an even more pressing financial position over the next 60 months—and that's *if* they manage to hold on to the car for that long.

Financially sound individuals may think examples like these are the exception, not the rule. They'll hear these kinds of scenarios and think I must be talking about a kid, a young adult who hasn't quite learned what it's like to experience the brunt of life's backlash. But they're absolutely wrong. I'm speaking of people in their 40s and 50s. People with children and grandchildren. People with degrees, who've held prestigious positions in the workplace. Believe me, financial irresponsibility is not limited to demographic differences like age, gender, or even race.

Despite my lack of amazement, I'll admit, it pains me each and every time. I hate to see people's lives succumb to the errs of a materialistic lifestyle. These lessons I share aren't intended to take you on an arbitrary trip down memory lane. I want you to realize what's possible when you prioritize your life around long-term objectives.

If you want something great—to see a difference in your life or with your finances—you have to give something up.

If you want a wife, you gotta give up the girl-friend-only lifestyle.

If you want the right to be selfish for the rest of your life, you'll have to give up certain ideals like marriage and children.

If you want to lose 30 lbs., that quart of ice cream you like to have as a midnight snack has to go. You gotta give up the excuses and hit the gym, too.

If you want to save money, give up those impulse buys and start giving some extra thought to your purchases.

If you want to retire without having to depend on Social Security benefits, stop financing your life on credit cards, and start planning those golden years.

Listen, I can carry on with these Ernest-isms all day long, but, as much as I know you enjoy hearing my two cents, I think you get the point. You have to be focused. You have to be committed! You have to want to see yourself reaching your goal more than anything.

To sum up my military experience, I kept up with my savings plan. Each month, I saw my savings grow higher than it's ever been. The only time I ever diverted from my strict savings goals was to make an investment in my desire to travel. After being so committed to my strategy and put-ting off a ton of opportunities to indulge, I think I earned the right to spend some time seeing the rest of the world. I took about two weeks off to tour Europe, visiting Amster-dam, London, Paris, Switzerland, and Italy along the way. Having dedicated two years to the military, I felt like that was more than enough time for me to fully appreciate the investment I made into myself and my future and enjoy a little TLC for a job well done. As frugal as I was, I realized that it is also important to take time to bask in the fruits of your labor and make "smart" investments with your money—investments that don't just satisfy you for a moment but the type that benefits your well-being and overall growth. Those tours were an experience, not a couple shots at the bar, a car I couldn't bring home, or a flashy new pair of Italian leather shoes. Those trips offered me memories that I'll hold on to forever.

We're human, so I get it. Desire is a natural thing. Still, you have to learn how to tame that desire, if you want to succeed. I showed discipline and prowess. I was beyond dedicated. By the time I was discharged from the military in January of 1990, I had approximately $10,500 in my savings account—and I was only 19 years old!

To date, I'd still say that was one of my greatest accomplishments. I never used my youth as an excuse. My lack of financial understanding didn't talk me out of the decision either. I knew what I wanted, and I did what I had to do to make it happen. It was uncomfortable at times. Sure, there were many "easier" options—but I made the decision that was best for me, a decision that would continue to serve me over the long-term.

To be honest, having money offers us a laundry list of benefits, some that can really place a twinkle in your eye, but, for me, it was the discipline that it took to save that money that really made me proud. I would go as far as to say that the discipline to save confers equal or greater value than the dollar itself, depending on how you look at the situation. Anyone can spend a dollar; it takes a focused individual to do what it takes to earn and save again.

I will say, we must respect life's seasons, and act accordingly. There are times when you'll be faced with a planting season, a time when you're called to store as much as you can, so those resources can accumulate and bear fruit. Then comes the harvest, the season where you're allowed to reap the bountiful benefits of all your hard work.

Seasons to save and seasons to invest. There'll be times in your life when circumstances prevent you from chucking huge sums of money into your savings. I understand that, as adults, it's nearly impossible for you to live on 20% of your income. Most will say they can barely live on 120% of their income as many survive by supplementing their income with debt. Even in those situations, savings should never be seen as an option or a bonus. At the very least, you should work to put away a minimum of $50 each month.

Master Plan: Number Three and Four

By the time it was all said and done, I was met with my own personal day of reckoning. I'll admit, my reasons for enlisting in the military were initially limited to its financial benefits, but, at the end of my term, I had been indelibly changed. The military turned me into a man, physically, mentally, and emotionally.

In January 1990, I was discharged from active duty. I boarded a plane, touching down to settle into the familiar basement in my parents' home. It took me a day or two to readjust to civilian life. All at once, there was no one around to bang on walls and trash cans to wake me up at the crack of dawn. No one to report to. Nothing to study. No platoon leaders and Drill Sergeants. Life at home was not the same either. Many of my high school classmates were hanging around, but that was because they'd recently flunked out of their freshman year of college. Those who had not elected to go to college were working in dead end jobs, if they even had a job at all. Even worse, the crack cocaine epidemic had officially crippled Chicago and all the neighboring towns, including ours.

I saw addicts walking the street, struggling to maintain consciousness through their drug-induced zombified state. Not to mention, many of my childhood friends had chosen to become drug dealers. Just like that, crack had become the cause and effect of the total transformation of everything I thought I knew. Day by day, I would learn of an old friend's "ascension" or descension into the destabilizing spiral this drug created. If my time in the military didn't leave me motivated enough, this rude awakening definitely got my attention. Seeing the effects of life on "the other side of the tracks" had me more focused than ever before. Crack caught my attention. I was scared straight, literally—and determined to continue to work to find my place in the world.

Working on the next stage in my plan, I got my brother Malcolm on the phone. I asked him for a ride to the Hyundai dealership, and he promised to swing by to pick me up. The next day, we took the short drive down the street, and I confidently walked onto the lot. Before I was discharged, I spent a year researching my options. Between budget and design, I already knew I'd be choosing a Hyundai. Stepping into the showroom, I laid eyes on a brand new blue car that lit up the whole room. My brother and I took turns circling the vehicle like sharks. We opened the doors, checked out the trunk, and took a look at the engine. We inspected every inch of the car. Then, I was faced with a tough decision.

No air! No power! No automatic anything. This car was as basic of a model as Hyundai could've created. The sticker had it priced at about $10,500. After some mild negotiations, we managed to talk the salesman down to $9,900 and I was on my way back out the door. I went straight to the bank to retrieve a cashier's check for $4,000.

I made my down payment and financed the balance, leaving the lot with a note of about $140 per month. All things considered, I was sure that car could get me through the next four years of college—the most recent amendment to my "master plan." (I'll touch on how that came about in just a second.) With that agreement, I finally achieved my third major life goal.

As fate would have it, a few weeks later, I met a young lady who was selling her motorcycle. It was a custom painted orange and blue Kawasaki EX250. It was love at first sight. She was asking three thousand dollars. I offered her two thousand five hundred dollars cash. Needless to say, I found myself back at the bank sooner than I thought. Just like that, all my hard work and savings had paid off. About $6,500 later, I had everything on my list, with money to spare.

Dreams do come true, folks—it just depends on how badly you want to make things happen. In the end, it wasn't the money or the things I purchased with the money that made that difference; it was the discipline, planning, sacrifice, and reward that made the difference. My military experience was the most transformative period of my life. It laid the foundation for everything to come. The military was also the worse experience of my life! I hated every minute of it. I think perhaps that is how "life goes." Growing pains are rarely, if ever, comfortable. Growth requires some level of discomfort.

If you are not uncomfortable, you are not growing!

Outtakes

Of Education

Claiming my seat in the second row of a small military classroom, I fixed my gaze upon a very large and imposing African American man. Our instructor, a Drill Sergeant like most other instructors, piqued my interest from his presence alone. I thought I was aptly prepared for anything he could throw. That is, until that imposing Drill Sergeant asked a question that I was not expecting at all.

"Who is going to college?"

More than half of the class raised their hands. My hand was nowhere to be found. There was no way I was going to college, so I thought. Sitting in that classroom, you couldn't have convinced me that I would ever set foot on a college campus—especially not Harvard. My master plan was clear and, unfortunately, college was nowhere on that list.

Settling in my seat, planting my feet firmly in my decision, the instructor's next question caught me by surprise.

"How many of you signed up for the GI Bill?"

This time, nearly every hand went soaring into the air. Every hand except mine and maybe three more people. He stops the class to look squarely at the four of us to strongly advise that we reconsider. When he uttered the words, "an education is very important," he didn't sound like a Drill Sergeant anymore. His tone wasn't stern, it was concerned, like a grandfather passing on profound wisdom. And, like most people who receive a lesson from experience, I disregarded it.

At the time, I didn't believe a word he said. I was not dissuaded, but I certainly believed he believed in what he was saying, I just didn't see things the same way. That didn't negate the concern that was written all over his face. And, to my surprise, the conversation didn't end there.

The four of us were later called into a small room adjoining the main classroom. Once inside, we were enveloped by three Drill Sergeants, all holding an intense look in their eyes.

"You all need to sign up for the GI Bill."

One of the four instantly caved, and he was allowed to leave on a promise to that he would. The sergeants pressed a bit harder, then a second guy decided to take heed to their advice. Now, all that were left were me and one other person.

The intervention continued:

"It's only $100 per month for 12 months. After you're discharged, you'll have $10,500 to use towards college," they said.

Finally I spoke up, "Sergeant, I am not going to college."

"Why? Why won't you sign up?"

I repeated my statement once more. "Sergeant, I am not going to college."

After what seemed like a lifetime, they shook their figurative heads at the only two holdouts and ushered us back into class. Then, someone said the words that still resound in my head until this day.

The largest sergeant in the group, standing there big and opposing, looked at us—maybe me, directly—to say:

"Son, you are about to make the biggest mistake of your life!"

No one ever knows when the words they've spoken or the time they spend with someone will change their lives forever. I'll always credit that man. He changed me for the better by speaking life into me; saying something I didn't even know I needed to hear. It was in that exact moment that an indelible seed was planted in my mind. For the first time in my life, I considered the idea that avoiding college could actually be a mistake—one that could cost me down the line.

So, my great awakening occurred almost in a flash while standing in formation.

Every day, we were woken up the same way, promptly at 5:30 a.m. Everything we did was like clockwork. On the days we did PT, we'd hear the order for long sleeve or short sleeve, shorts or sweat pants. Our uniforms were always ordained. On non-PT days, we'd hear someone bark summer BDUs or winter BDUs, a heavier uniform. The weather would only change the attire, but we were always woken up to a parade of yelling and banging on garbage cans—rain, snow, sleet, or shine.

Let me tell you right now, I hated it all. Being woken up to people running down the halls, beating on the doors, bursting into our rooms, shouting at the tops of their lungs was not my idea of a good time. I dreaded the sound every time I went to sleep at night. By the time morning came, and I found myself being awakened by the sound of the rapture, I'd be so groggy and disoriented. Begrudgingly getting dressed and scurrying down two flights of stairs, I assumed my place in line.

The squad leader would look down the line to make certain we were all accounted for and in the proper uniform. The platoon leader would harken out the command: "Platoon, Attention!" Like a well-oiled machine, we'd all snap into formation. Arms straight. Fingers curled. Arms stretched to our side, pressed into our legs.

If you aren't familiar with the military, let me walk you through our system, just so you can follow along a little better.

- I am the soldier.
- Soldiers are one of 7–8 other soldiers in what's known as a "squad".
- The squad is one of 4–5 other squads that comprise our platoon.
- The platoon is one of four other platoons, and, together, we make up a company.
- The company is one of several other companies within the same battalion.

And that, my friends, is a snapshot of the matrix that is our great military.

Squad leaders were the enlisted men with the highest ranking. We were led by a platoon leader with 15 or so years of tenure. His superior, on the other hand, was an officer with just two years of service—not much more than me, actually. Our regimen leader was a First Sergeant with maybe 16 years of military service, and his boss, the Captain, became an officer after approximately five years. It did not take me very long to figure out the existing dynamic. Enlisted men were the most respected, but they weren't the ones who called the shots. The officers were in charge.

I found myself questioning if there was something that all of the officers had in common. Then, I realized the answer—education. To be an officer, you were required to have a bachelor's degree, at minimum. That revelation altered everything I thought I felt about going to college. I never wanted to spend another day standing in formation. I was ready to sign on the dotted line.

I wanted to be the man standing in front of the regimen or the man leading the battalion. Education was the key to creating a clear pathway to turn that dream into reality. Except, I had one slight problem. Mr. Stuck-In-His-Ways never signed up for the GI Bill.

My heart sank. I felt an unsettling panic come across my body. Oh, my God! I wrote him off as overzealous and a bit misguided, but that Drill Sergeant was right. I really made one of the worst mistakes of my life.

As I'm writing this, my mind travels back to that classroom; back to the moment where I stubbornly stood against his pleas. Then, I flash back to the time where I found myself standing in formation having one of those famous Oprah "aha" moments. I had missed my opportunity to sign up for the GI Bill. As a matter of fact, I threw the opportunity away. I had a very simple plan to kickstart my life, and, after holding on to it for so long, I never considered the need to revise or adjust it in anyway. I was only 17 when I placed myself in a man's world. I didn't know anything about going to college, particularly about the ways people financed their education. Standing in that line, only one thing was clear. I missed an opportunity to receive $10,000 towards the cost of my tuition.

Wallowing in despair over the next month, I didn't know what to do. I was a very forward, direct young man. Normally, when my mind was made up, I made things happen. Refusing to take heed to wise counsel, I found myself faced with a brick wall. That is, until one glorious day. Well, it didn't begin very gloriously, especially not with our usual banging and screaming routine. But, once we were in line, something changed soon after Sergeant Manes walked in front of the platoon.

"At ease! At ease." Upon his command, every soldier responded by placing our hands on the smalls of our backs, pivoting on our right foot, and standing in still silence.

"If anyone has not signed up for the GI Bill by now, there is a three-month amnesty period. You have three months from this day to sign up," he continued.

It seemed as if his words opened up the gates of heaven, and I could see the silhouette of the face of God. Without hesitation, I signed up. I didn't even have to wait to commence my education, they were already offering a few courses on base. I enrolled in The Psychology of Dreaming; Sigmund Freud, the first of many courses to come.

Military offerings allowed me to complete enough courses to earn credits for a half-year of college. Knowing my options were limited, I spent my evenings researching schools I could attend after I was discharged. I learned that Senator Paul Simon, of Illinois, was a veteran and Veteran

Advocate. The State of Illinois was actually one of a handful of states that provided opportunities for returning veterans to attend a public university for free. The Illinois Veteran Grant Program offered us tuition-free enrollment in addition to the monies I was set to receive from the GI Bill. So, my plan adjusted.

I decided to earn as many college credits as I could while I was in the military, then I'd enroll in a public university in Illinois to take advantage of the benefits posed by the grant program. My research helped me narrow down my choices to two institutions: Chicago State University and the University of Illinois-Champaign. In the end, Chicago State won the bid because I wanted to be at home (free room and board) and have an opportunity to experience life in Chicago as a young adult with a few nice resources. On top of it all, outside of kindergarten, I always attended schools that made me the minority. This time around, I wanted the chance to go to a school where African Americans were the majority. I was sure Chicago State could offer me quite the experience. Just like that, my mind was made up.

College became my next mission, almost an obsession for me. With a little more than a year to prepare for my next phase in life, I had a lot of time to think. I realized that I tended to lean towards a specific pattern of behavior. Whenever I was in one phase, I was already preparing for the next. Then, I'd devise a plan and execute.

I always knew it would take time to reach my goals; nothing ever happens overnight, nothing worthwhile anyway. When I was in high school, I kept my plan in my right pocket for almost a year. It took me two years to execute the first two things I had on that list. This next phase of my life, the college phase, was going to require at least a four-year commitment.

Of Racism

I touched down in July of 1988 at my permanent duty station, Fulda, West Germany. Fulda is a small city approximately five kilometers from the East German border. At the time it was occupied by Russian soldiers. Upon arrival, I was processed and assigned a room in the barracks. I was led up the stairs to the third floor. The door flung open, and I was directed to the bottom bunk of two bunkbeds crammed into the space. On the far side of the room, there was an empty single bed. Judging by the layout, I expected there'd be five of us sharing the room.

Before long, I met one of my roommates, a black guy from Virginia. He was a "lifer," a title given to people whose primary intention is to retire in the military. Another was an older white man who was waiting to be medically discharged. "Hands," we called him, since his age and years of labor left him to deal with a few issues with his right hand. Then, there was Kendall, the trouble maker. I could tell he wasn't long from being kicked out of the military. Disobeying orders and playing by your own rules was the easiest way to be dishonorably discharged.

Lastly, there was Bores from Nebraska. The guy who "didn't like niggers"—which happened to be one of the first things he said to me. The self-proclaimed Klansman said he'd never seen a black person until he enlisted. I'm not sure if I believe him. I doubt he'd interacted with many black people in Nebraska in the 80s but to say he'd never laid eyes on one of us seems to be a bit of a stretch.

Nevertheless, Bores and I were constantly at odds. He wasn't shy about expressing his disdain for black people, and I was never shy about reminding him how prepared I was to render him unconscious. We seemed to be trapped in that roundabout shuffle. Two posturing young men, filled with aggression, fueled by testosterone. Outside of exchanging verbal blows, things rarely got more physical than a push or stiff brush of the shoulder before our roommates would break things up.

Racism was not new to me. After we moved from the projects in the South Side of Chicago to the suburbs, there were many days when I'd hear, "Nigger!" before dodging some random article that was tossed from a speeding car. It seemed like a weekly occurrence, back then—so Bores wasn't anyone I didn't know how to deal with. In the past, my response was usually riddled with a slew of profanity-laced comebacks followed by the projection of the nearest rock or stick, anything I could hurl back at the vehicle.

Just in case they circled back around, I'd arm myself with a big stick or something to defend myself. If the vehicle happened to hit the brakes or begin to back up, I'd take off like a rocket. Even as a child, I was fast, very fast. I was never worried about being caught. I knew every street, path, and shortcut like the back of my hand. I even taught myself the route to my friends' houses, just in case. I knew all the houses to avoid because they had dogs in the backyard or, more commonly, because they "didn't like black people." I knew all the houses that could provide me a safe haven. From an early age, an unwitting relationship with racism taught me to adapt to my surroundings and respond appropriately. So, Bores was the last of my worries.

I remember one time, a Saturday, when I was thrust back into that same old shuffle. I was in high school by then, and pretty seasoned in racial affairs. A car drove by me, stopping about half a block up the street. One of the passengers screamed out, "Nigger!"

Without hesitation, "Cracker" and the f-bomb flew out of my mouth. The next thing I heard was burning tires. The car was already in reverse and speeding my way. Like lightning, I was gone—I'd took off running! I never looked back.

A couple days later, I was back in school standing at the lockers, and one of my friends came up to me laughing. He only lived about a block from my home, so we met each other around the neighborhood.

"Ditto! That was me in the car the other day. I told them you would say something if they called you a name."

I cracked up laughing too.

Even with the dynamic of race; more specifically, racism proving to be such a sensitive topic, things were different while I was in high school. Standing in the bunker, enlisted in the military alongside men like Bores, that created an entirely different situation.

Growing up in these types of environments made me sensitive to topics like race and color. The environment made me feel like I needed to prove myself as a black man living in a dominant white male society. The world made me feel as if I was a problem to be solved, like I could only be valuable if I was the "token" smart one.

I had to prove my humanity and fight for my respect. I had to work twice as hard to stand my ground against that level of opposition. And, with all that said, I was ready for however anyone wanted to handle those tense situations, especially Bores.

As they say, when life gives you lemons, make lemonade. After a crash-course on the type of culture I signed into, I decided to make lemonade, lemon pies, lemon cakes, and lemon drops very early on.

Chapter 6

Beyond the Closed Doors: Harvard

Remember when the Clampett's struck oil? Who didn't love Granny, Jed, Jethro and Elly May? At the very least you had to love the song! Well, I had a similar song, when I struck my proverbial "black gold. Texas tea." I am clearing my throat; please feel free to sing along with me:

Their version:

"Come and listen to my story about a man named Jed
A poor mountaineer, barely kept his family fed,
And then one day he was shootin' at some food,
And up through the ground come a bubblin' crude.

Oil that is, black gold, Texas tea.

Well the first thing you know ol' Jed's a millionaire,
The kinfolk said 'Jed move away from there'
Said 'Californy is the place you ought to be'
So they loaded up the truck and they moved to Beverly

Hills, that is. Swimmin' pools, movie stars.

The Beverly Hillbillies"

My version:

"Let me tell you a story of Ernest with a Father named Red,
a Chicago Born kid, cash poor but well read,
And one day he applied to law school,

And in from the mail gotta an offer or two.
Law School that is, THE American Dream.
Well the next thing you know Old Ernest is Ivy League,
The kinfolk said go make your family proud,
Said Harvard Law is the place you ought to be,
So I loaded up the Accord and drove to the East.
East Coast that is, Charles River and MIT.
Class of 1997"

Aaannd Bow......Thank You!

Well, in place of the pickup truck, I loaded up the Honda Accord and made my way to Cambridge. I arrived a few weeks early. I wanted to find an apartment off campus. My best friend in college, James, who took the drive with me, had relatives who allowed me to live with them for free until I found an apartment.

I spent my days searching for a place in Somerville, Massachusetts, which was a much more affordable neighborhood for me than Cambridge. There weren't more than a handful of students on campus when I arrived. More began to sprinkle in about two weeks out. The first marker of my experience as a student is my memory of being on my second read of *Race Matters* by Cornel West. Cornel West is a former professor at Princeton, Yale, and Harvard—perhaps the most preeminent scholar on race at the time. To be honest, I only understood about every other word written in his book on my first go around. Blown away by his use of language and the way his intelligence jumped off the page, Dr. West left me intrigued, to say the least. Strolling across the campus yard, I walked through the grass until a line of trees came into sight. I noticed a flyer hanging from a tree:

"Cornel West at Ames Hall. Today at 3 PM."

The surge of excitement that flowed through my veins was almost the equivalent of the release of Purple Rain. If you could've felt what I felt in that moment, you would've thought that sign read:

"Free Prince Concert Tonight—Front Row Seats with This Flyer!"

Ok, maybe I'm exaggerating a little, but you have to understand how overwhelming it was.

I got to the hall about 15 minutes early. Walking into such an old, non-descript building was my second memory. You would think a place like Harvard with the prestige and esteem would be lined with state-of-the-art, top-of-the-line facilities. As the young folk say: NOT. They were stuck in the Paper Chase Era, dotted with old, gloomy buildings. The Law School countered its 5-star reputation with 3-star accommodations you'd expect to see at the end of an old country dirt road. I learned that you had to visit the Business School to see what good living was like. But I digress— back to the honorable Dr. West.

The flyer directed me to a grim, outdated classroom designed with tiered seating. There weren't more than 30 chairs in the space, most of which would remain unfilled. A few minutes later, the great mind from the book walked into the room. Dr. Cornel West made his entrance, and I gave him my undivided attention for the next hour. We listened to him speak and follow up with a Q & A session. It was an enriching exchange, one I didn't quite expect at Harvard.

It was the spring of 1994. There I was, an enthusiastic "1L" at Harvard Law School. I felt like the world was at my fingertips.

In the spring, the campus is filled with chatter and excitement. At any given moment, you could find yourself standing next to an officer in the military, a valedictorian from MIT, or someone working on a joint MBA from the

Business School and a JD from Harvard Law. You'd meet the sons and daughters of Congressman and the heirs to billion-dollar estates. This person's father is one of the largest developers in New York and that person's father owns a bank. You'd hear casual conversations, "Both my parents are doctors, but I decided on law school. My sister is in medical school." To put matters into perspective, the landmark case desegregating public schools in 1954, Brown v. Board of Education, was only forty years removed from my first year in law school, yet several of my African American classmates were second generation graduates of the Law School. This was startling to me. My brain was on overload.

Approximately one-third of the class attended Harvard undergrad; another twenty percent were legacy students (their parents attended); another twenty percent or so attended other Ivy League schools; ten percent or so were African American. That's too when I learned "Affirmative Action" came in many forms that extend well beyond race, and access and opportunity is not purely based on a meritocracy. I'd gladly trade in my black "Affirmative Action" for legacy "Affirmative Action" or wealthy parent "Affirmative Action." I'm not suggesting anyone was undeserving of admittance; I'm simply suggesting there are factors beyond test scores and undergraduate class rank that factored into the selection process (my humble belief). And there's most certainly a diversity formula that went well beyond color.

In March 2019, as I am putting the finishing touches on this book, the United States federal prosecutors detail a college admissions bribery scandal. Operation Varsity Blues, as it is nicknamed, details allegations of bribery of school administrators, inflation of test scores, cheating on SAT and ACT tests, and handing out scholastic scholarships to non-athletes. All paid for by wealthy white families for the benefit of their already privileged children in order to gain entrance into universities such as Yale, Stanford, Georgetown, and the University of Southern California. This is wrong on so many levels. The wealth advantage was not enough; the famous advantage was not enough; and the white in America advantage was not enough. They want it all! Another lesson I've learned, the elite are not interested in winning. The elite are interested in complete domination and control. They want every advantage. They want all the money. They want to own all the businesses. They have little or no mercy.

Anyhow, my experience at the time provided a priceless firsthand glimpse into the power and advantage of privilege. What they spoke casually about, I never even imagined. Fine, I watched The Jefferson's. I knew George was successful. I knew he had "moved on up." I was unaware all of this existed. Yea yea, I watched every episode of The Cosby Show. Claire was a lawyer and Bill was a doctor, but it never occurred to me this existed in real life.

The gift I was provided is the knowing ***impossible is possible!***

I'd imagine Barack Obama learned a similar lesson there too. That type of environment utilizes doubt as fertilizer for whatever possibility you may dare to imagine.

This is why it is so important to travel and be exposed to different people and environments. They are "the gifts that keep on giving." And it goes well beyond education. Confidence, perspective, and possibility are as integral to success as the nuts and bolts of education or the black letter of the law. Although many despise acknowledging Donald Trump for anything, or not much at all, I must say the man "believes in himself" and thinks "big." And, sometimes, belief in one self and thinking "big" is the difference!

At first glance, Harvard presented a very intimidating environment. You'd regularly taste the question, "Am I good enough?" floating through the air. The time it crossed my mind was inevitable, just like everyone else who stepped foot on that campus. It didn't matter where they came from or what they were meant to inherit, just about everyone at Harvard found themselves in awe at the idea that they were actually accepted and attending the renowned institution it is. I don't think that sense ever wears off.

Well, once the allure settles a bit, it's settle in and focus time.

First year students had the opportunity to work at a corporate law firm. There was essentially a perfect intern placement rate for interested students. When you're a student at an Ivy League school, your dilemmas are different. Planning for your future was less of a question of finding a position and more like, "should I intern with my first, second, or third choice of firms?" First year doubled as a professional head start, since corporate law was likely the eventual career path of most. Aside from the possibility of securing an internship with one of the best law firms in the country, there came an ungodly salary. We're talking ranges between $5,000–$6,000 per month. And that was before you accepted a formal offer. As a 24-year-old young man, the spring of 1994 gave me a different view of the world.

I must admit, back then, I struggled to wrap my brain around the value I could offer a company that would warrant such a tremendous salary. I was still a first year student; I had to find myself. Now, I chuckle every time I think back on the man I once was. It's amazing to see how far you can come, just by recognizing who you are. It's even more interesting to see how much you change after learning the way the world works. Imagine the shock on my face after someone explained that we weren't paid that huge chunk of money as interns because the firm expected us to earn it. Those large 1st-year stipends were the firm's way of making sure that they stayed in our good graces. That paid internship was just the employer's way of buying their way into first place, so they could have access to the school's best talent pool. You know, for future recruitment.

Now, *that* made sense. If only someone would've told me that earlier on in life. They could've made it simple for us. I would've appreciated an analogy like "Oh, this internship is something like what happens when a young NBA prospect receives an endorsement deal with Nike before they ever step foot on a NBA court." Then, I would've understood exactly the way things worked.

Alas, I had to feel things out for myself.

That process taught me another very important lesson: there are a lot of perks at the "top." Reminiscing places a sinister grin on my face. Excuse me, but I can't help but laugh at this. People with money really know how to pull out all the stops to get what they want.

Even with a fat check sitting on the table, as fate would have it, I decided to spend my summer carving my own path. Ole' genius me decides to forego the cushy internship at a big shot law firm. I told them they could keep their $15,000. I stood on my soapbox and said, "You can't entice me with your white-glove catered lunches, car service, and ridiculously large paydays." I was a man on a mission, a man with principle and conviction.

Are you kidding me? I was insane.

Can you hear the anguish I still maintain? I'm sure my pain and frustration are coming through on this page. To this day, I wonder how my life would have changed. What would have been different for me, if I decided to ignore the warnings of my moral compass and just took the bait?

I can imagine a fantastic, gluttonous lifestyle. I probably would've become this high-rolling bigwig attorney.

Stepping into the courtroom with flashy black and blue pinstripe suits. I could've had a closet bursting at the seams with tailored ensembles, embroidered shirts, and anything else I could dream up. Shoes made from imported Italian leather. Ah, man! The shiny black Bostonians I could have collected. The dinners, the prestige, the pride I could have brought to my parents. I could've used my position to place a spotlight on my family's name. I have these thoughts from time to time, then my bubble's burst when I come back to reality. All those possibilities went down the drain that year. Even when I'm temporarily stopped with regret, I get it.

I made my bed, I have to lie in it.

I was friends with a colorful character named Maury in my Harvard days. Maury summed up something important for me, in a way that only he could. One day, he grabbed me by the shoulder and laid it on thick! He said, "Ernest, bruh! Let me ask you this. What the hell is Chicago State? Look, I'm going down the list—we've got Harvard, Princeton, Yale, Columbia, Duke, Morehouse, and...Chicago State? Bruh. Chicago State."

After his taunts, he shed light on something I'd never forget. He said, "Out of everyone here, I'm most impressed by you. It's not where you are, it's the distance you've travelled!" long exaggerated pause.... "And bruh, you've come a long way."

I knew I was the only graduate of Chicago State University to be accepted into Harvard Law School. Unfortunately, I am still the only person some 25 years later. Yet, I never thought about it in that way. I was accustomed to doing things first. I seemed to always be travelling a long way. My parents travelled a long way from Mississippi to Chicago with three children in the late nineteen sixties while in their early twenties—a much greater distance travelled than mine.

I'd like to think my military training served me well in preparing me for the culture at Harvard. Hearing Maury's words helped me find confidence in knowing that, of all the people there, all those who'd been guaranteed seats thanks to their family's donations and their pedigree, I'd travelled farther than most of them. Even without Congressman and Wall Street traders to list on my application, I made it to Harvard just the same.

That's when I learned that Harvard was going to be whatever I decided to make it. If I made it "this far" through improvisation that would make John Coltrane himself proud, my potential was unlimited at this stage.

It's not where you are that defines you, it's the distance travelled.

O.J. and the Bronco

Then, scandal hit. Not scandal in the school, scandal that shook the nation to its core. When that white Bronco was plastered across the screen, O.J. Simpson created "breaking news" that impacted my Harvard experience. Ironically enough, my first year in law school and the infamous O.J. Simpson trial for the murder of Nicole Brown were concurrent.

That Bronco chase aired live in 1994, and the People of the State of California v. Orenthal James Simpson began in January of 1995. News cameras made their way to campus every day of the trial. CNN regularly interviewed students to get our insight. I remember learning that two professors from the Law School, Charles Ogletree and Alan Dershowitz, were part of his legal team. Both of these men happened to be common fixtures around campus, which made them an essential addition to the student experience. I had the privilege of hearing each of them lecture on more than one occasion. Before long, the O.J. case became a part of our curriculum.

Judge Ito, the judge assigned to the case, consulted with my first year Criminal Law class. He requested we provide pro and con briefs on the issue of admissibility into evidence of the 911-emergency call made by Nicole Brown. The issue was whether the "probative" value of the tapes would outweigh the potential "prejudicial" effect it may have on jurors (the tapes were ultimately allowed to be played to the jurors). Just like that, we were moved way beyond the limits of lectures and hypotheticals, we were handling real issues and our contributions were impacting current events. In fact, the judge personally thanked our class for our contributions on CNN, after it was made known that the tapes would be allowed. That, my friends, showed me the influence of Harvard Law.

On October 3, 1995, O.J. was acquitted with the same publicity used to spotlight his entire trial. I can remember standing outside of the cafeteria watching the verdict on screen. Like the rest of America, every person on campus was glued to a television. When the ruling was announced, there was an instant divide. The African American students cheered. The white students screamed, some even cursed, and many others broke out in tears. That was Harvard as well.

Although we had many commonalities, nothing could overcome the racial disparity and dissension many of us endured. One of the most notable points about that verdict was the glaring division it sparked along racial lines. When Los Angeles County residents were polled for their opinions on the decision, most of the African American population felt justice had been served by the "not guilty" verdict, while the white and Latino majority disagreed.

Although Harvard set us apart from the masses in many ways, cases like the O.J. Simpson trial proved we weren't really removed from society.

Those first two years at Harvard offered insight into exactly where I was. It helped me understand more about the culture and appreciate all I'd done to earn my position amongst the who's who of the academic sphere. Despite racial divide in the nation, I was enrolled alongside people of every race, color, and creed.

By year three, I learned to master the formula that would help me succeed. After moving on campus for the third year, I had to figure out how to maintain balance between school and my entrepreneurial career. (Oh yea, I'll share more about my first formal business venture in the chapters to come.) My business was growing and the demand for me to be in the store and "on the ground" was growing along with it. I found myself on a plane flying back and forth between Chicago and Cambridge almost weekly, since the beginning of my second year. Four days in Chi Town and three days at school, then rotate the following week.

The mental anguish of first and second year had largely dissipated. I knew what to expect now. I understood how to take tests, pace myself, and relax under the pressure of exams.

By then, the utter amazement of my classmates backgrounds, having celebrities visit campus in tourist-like fashion, sitting in on lectures with consumer and civil rights advocates like Ralph Nader and Dick Gregory, hearing about a brilliant female professor on campus, Elizabeth Warren, and being introduced in an almost folklore fashion to this guy named Barack Obama, who was the first African American named President of Harvard Law Review, was all beginning to become my new normal.

I am being groomed to be great TOO.

I am one of the chosen ones TOO.

From the very beginning we were told, "you all represent the best and brightest the world has to offer. You represent the top one percent from every background. Of all the students in the world, you sit atop of all of them here at Harvard Law. So, even if you find yourself at the bottom of the class, you are still atop 99% of everyone else. At worse, you are still 'the bottom of the top.'"

They were essentially insulating us from the possibility of failure. It even went beyond that, they were essentially saying, "even if you find yourself at the bottom of your class, you are still the best."

Think about the power of that for a moment.

And juxtapose the promise of that messaging against the backdrop of the messaging young black men all across America receive from almost every other institution they encounter.

TV: dope dealers.

Music: gangstas

News: criminals.

Education: dropouts and Attention Deficit Disorder (ADD).

Medical: high risk diabetic, heart disease, and cancer. The first to DIE.

At all times you are being indoctrinated. Indoctrinated to rule or to be ruled, but indoctrinated nonetheless!

What if the narrative were re-written? What if young men like me were told of their greatest potential? And that potential was cultivated.

What "got me" to Harvard despite the direct or indirect attempts at negatively indoctrinating me is *I learned to tell myself stories that had me winning!*

"Learn to Tell Yourself Stories that Have You Winning!" no matter what how others may attempt to discredit you or your ideas.

Learn to Tell Yourself Stories that Have You Winning, even when you are not quite certain how you will accomplish your own goals.

You don't have to be a student at Harvard. Learn to Affirm your Greatness. AND then follow it up with Action!

Remember, Ms. Smith told me, "if someone asks you what you want, you tell them!" Well, that lesson was appropriate here too; when they told me I was special, "I believed them!" Not without struggle, however. My battle as an African American man, in particular, was in my ability to reconcile the Southside of Chicago "me" with the Ivy League "me." The kid who washed his jeans in the sink "me," with the young man purchasing Bostonian wing tips "me." The standing in line at McDonald's "me," with the white linen dinner events "me."

The greatest conflict was not the daunting work load, but the burden of shifting the resounding narrative in my head of what it means to be Black, a young man, and on the lower economic scale in America! This is where many of us lose: in our heads. Long before we enter Harvard or high school. We lose the psychological war between doubt and ability; the war between true community ownership and temporary leaseholds; being honored as a contribution in the room and being locked out of the room; and being prepared to excel AS WE ARE and subsisting in a form others desire we are.

I had to resolve the conflict of being a black man in what has historically been hostile institutions to my forefathers: the legal system, wealth, privilege, education. If you thought the coursework was difficult, try solving all of that and staying focused while preparing for exams! My struggle with reconciling my two selves (Du Bois again) was most challenged in law school! I was struggling emotionally. There was a cultural and spiritual warring world, inside me!

Take a deep breath. Relax. Remember my purpose. Game face on. Go!

That is why I chose them: a look behind the "closed doors."

Fail Forward.

Find a Competitive Advantage and Hard Work: Dedication

Finding a Competitive Advantage

The thought of law school was as probable for me as was Barack Hussein Obama being elected President of the United States of America, prior to him winning Ohio in the primary. I'm the guy it took a team of Drill Sergeants and what seemed like torture at the time, with me standing in formation in below freezing temperatures, to be persuaded of the value of college. It was only then I saw the metaphorical "light" of pursuing a degree. I guess my mother was right again, "a hard head makes a soft tail."

After all it took to get me to college, I was confronted with yet another uncomfortable reality when I was near graduation: a bachelor's degree may not "be enough!"

Lord, help me.

I'll be damned, by junior year of college, I was beginning to think a bachelor's degree was not enough.

Why didn't anyone tell me a bachelor's degree at the time would not assuage my ambitions? They said college! No one ever said a master's degree or PhD. And I had no idea what a Juris Doctorate was at the time—still not quite certain.

My major was Business Management. My plan was to one day become an entrepreneur after working in Corporate America. Problem was, Chicago State University, at best, positioned me to compete for a low- to low-mid-level management position. That's the military version of being a low- to mid-level ranked enlisted soldier. I'd be in formation again. In the cold. Looking at the officers strut in front of formation while barking out orders at me. I was not having that again. Look, I know, it's honorable to serve in the military and graduate and take a position in a company and work your way up—just not for me.

Alright fine: now what? So, again, I retreated to the internal debate we all have from time to time: "So, you say you want more. What are you going to do about it? It's not fair. Who said anything about life being fair?"

That's how life comes at you. Life, "You want something from me? Are you willing to pay the price?"

Life requires currency when you ask something of it. It is the price one must pay.

One of the great poets of our time espoused: "Hard Work; Dedication! Hard Work; Easy Work!" The message being he makes what is hard work to others easy for him, albeit through hard work! Oh yea, the great poet is Floyd Mayweather. (Don't judge me!) Floyd is not exactly the first person you would think of when imagining prophetic life advice or prose, but his words are powerful. Dedication and hard work makes what is hard work easy work. If it is hard for others and easy to me, I'll be better prepared. And the challenge or "work" of competing against you becomes easy. That's it.

That sounds all good, yet I was transported back to the fifteen-year-old me. Holding another sit-in. This time it wouldn't be about my parents' failure to assuage me with new clothes at the beginning of the school year. This time my demise would be my own doing. I was willfully setting myself up for disappointment. I could just imagine me sitting in an uncomfortable cubicle in a gray room with no windows. A demure and squeaky voiced boss barking out orders at me this time in place of the Drill Sergeant. "Fenton, if you want to be the boss, you should have gotten a master's degree like me. NOW! Where is my report!"

Absolutely not! This cannot be my destiny.

I was at a crossroads in my life once again. What would be my next move?

Since my plan was to become a business man, an MBA was most logical. I began researching business schools and their admission criteria. All of the top tier business schools required two years of work experience. I figured military would count as work experience. As I looked into business school and its curriculum further, it wasn't too different than what I already studied: accounting, economics, statistics, strategic management, business management. I'm thinking, "I don't need business school to learn how to do business." I was confident I could learn business on my own and had enough foundation in business to be successful. Business was natural to me. I had been a budding business man since I was fourteen years of age, shoveling driveways, mowing lawns and cutting trees with my father in his business.

"What will separate me from everyone else? What would position me to have a seat at almost any table?"

Eureka: law school! (I did not say, "Eureka," I just like the way it sounds.)

It came to me almost from out of nowhere. I had never considered law school until that moment.

If you want something great or extraordinary, you gotta be prepared to do something great and be extraordinary. Then the doubters emerged. Why are you going to law school? Aren't there enough lawyers? Do you really want to practice law? You're going to do another three years of college? Are you going to stay in school forever? My answer was always the same:

"I'm going to law school to become smarter."

Folk thought I was crazy, again!

What type of mumbo jumbo answer was that? Who pays one hundred thousand dollars and invests three years of their life to "get smarter?"

For me it was an opportunity to gain a competitive intellectual advantage over my peers. I wanted to be the smartest person in the room.

I wanted to be the best prepared in any professional endeavor.

I attended law school to learn to think. I desired the mental edge I believed law school could assist in cultivating in me.

I decided on law school for a few reasons; what was most odd to almost everyone with the exception of me is that I did not attend law school to become a lawyer.

There were no lawyers in my family. To this day, I am the only one. I had no personal relationships with lawyers. I had no idea of what law school entailed. I just believed the knowledge I would acquire would be transferrable. And, I figured being a lawyer could open doors for me.

My newly devised path required I be accepted into a top tier law school or Howard University. I figured If I could not attend a top tier law school, then I'd as soon attend Howard, an HBCU. Either I'm going to "play with the big boys," or I was going to enjoy myself while being educated at Howard. So, it was attending a top tier law school (top twenty law schools in the country) or Howard; that's it.

I immersed myself in books about law school. I purchased every study guide known to mankind. I enrolled in a law school admission test (LSAT) class and I carried the study guide around with me for six months. Every day I would study. In between classes, I studied. At home on the weekends, I studied. On summer break while working as a Cook County Life Guard, I'd study in between shifts. I was relentless in my pursuit to be accepted into a top tier law school.

One of my proudest accomplishments was being accepted into Howard and offered a full ride. I had a few other offers for full ride scholarships too. About the same time I was sorting through my options, I received an acceptance letter from Harvard Law School. No money. Just an opportunity to attend. Here's the dilemma, "Do I take the full ride to Howard, or pay six figures to attend Harvard?" Well, I guess you know which I chose.

Sometimes, you gotta pay to play!

I learned later in life, just because something is free, doesn't mean there's no cost. And just because something costs, doesn't mean it doesn't pay!

Ultimately, however, what set me on fire was the thought of being able to compete against the best and brightest. That was a priceless opportunity.

Howard would have been comfortable, and I wasn't seeking comfort. I was seeking to find what I was made of!

Of Hard Work

It was about 9 a.m. A day seared in my memory. I was walking past the Reginald Lewis International Law Library. I didn't know who Reginald Lewis was. I knew all about his $5 million dollar donation, though. At the time, it was the largest single donation ever made to Harvard Law School. That's what got him his own library.

An alumni of the school, Reginald Lewis amassed his fortune on Wall Street. He was the first African American to close a billion dollar overseas leveraged buyout deal. He also was the first and only person to be accepted into Harvard Law School without applying. Curiosity led me to his book, *Why Should White Guys Have All the Fun?* It was awe inspiring, to say the least. But that isn't what grasped at me on that Saturday morning.

Peering through the window, I noticed a table of about eight Asian students studying away. It wouldn't have been so unusual, but, for one, it was first thing in the morning on a Saturday, and two, our only tests were at least three months away.

I thought to myself, "They must be getting a jump on things…"

Dismissing the sight, I headed to the gym for about an hour and a half. On my way back to the dorm, I walked by that same window, and the group was still in there, heads down, buried in their textbooks.

Now, I'm thinking, "That's impressive."

Still, it was a fleeting thought. I went to hang out in my room. Probably watched a little television, washed clothes—all the typical Saturday morning stuff. I left back out around one o'clock in the afternoon to go have lunch. Eat my food, chat with friends, and then, as I'm leaving the cafeteria, I walk past the library again at around 2:30 p.m. I just happened to look over and what I saw shocked me to the core. By this point, I'd gone through a whole day and completely forgot about that study group. To my surprise, they were still in there, sitting at that table with their heads in the books.

Now, that was Harvard!

Maybe two weeks into the year, those Asian students spent a minimum of seven hours studying in the library that Saturday and many Saturdays after that. Some would say it was "too early," but Harvard taught me the importance of going above and beyond.

If you want what others don't have, you have to do what others aren't willing to do. Harvard taught me to never get comfortable with where I was because, somewhere out there, there would always be someone willing to work twice as hard.

So, what was it like to attend Harvard? Eye-opening, to say the least. Harvard showed me the level of commitment that was necessary for success. It taught me the world was filled with extremely motivated and brilliant people.

Harvard opened my eyes to so many different narratives. It taught me how to unlearn the half-truths that are taught to us about race, success, and opportunity. I had to go to Harvard to learn that all black people don't share the same "rags to riches" story. I had to be at Harvard to receive a firsthand lesson on the work ethic of silver spoon babies— some of them work harder than you could ever imagine.

I had to attend Harvard to learn that, while wrapped in a world sustained by a myriad of people who'd come from all different backgrounds, *I belonged.*

If I could belong in Harvard, competing and exceling in various ways, then Harvard had room for more people like me. All you have to do is seize the opportunity and find your place in your "Harvard."

Chapter 7

So You Say You Want to Be an Entrepreneur?

The Ivy League Law School graduate decides he doesn't want to cash the "golden ticket" and practice law. What did I do instead? I'm sure you're dying to know. What in the world was more important to me than free money, a guaranteed job, and a summer filled with unending bribery?

Volunteering.

You read that correctly. I decided that I wanted to volunteer instead. Oh, so now you're the one who's laughing, I guess.

I went with being a volunteer over being paid for my compliance. While my already-richer-than-me peers went off to live the good life, I wasn't paid a dime. Nothing. Nada.

It was yet another defining moment in my life. To this day, I sincerely believe that decision became the very moment I changed the pathway of my life.

When my mind was made up, I visited one of the most preeminent legal scholars in the country, who also happened to be a professor at Harvard, Charles Ogletree. During our meeting, I shared my interest with Professor Ogletree, confessing that I was not interested in slaving away on a corporate farm.

Yeah, I was that kid. The visionary. The revolutionary. The rule-breaker. Although it was clear that there was an established order amongst my peers, I didn't envision myself working at a sterile law firm. I never liked the idea of being forced to laugh at corny jokes or spending my days listening to recycled presentations about the grandeur of this "great opportunity." The merry-go-round sing-song never appealed to me.

If you've never heard it before, it goes something like:

*"We here at XYZ firm are *insert inflated mission statement*. Our founders were *insert fabricated tale of brave heroics*.*

(Cue the list of prestigious partners and associates)

*These people went on to *insert philanthropic tale of corporate success*.*

And, if you don't die en route, you will make millions of dollars as a partner after eight years of doing twenty years of work.

You want to thank me now or later?

On your way out, please leave a pint of blood at the front desk—just in case."

Well, I may have exaggerated this just a little, but, in my mind, it sounded just like this—maybe even worse, to be honest.

After buying into the notion that I was an exceptional blue-chip recruit, I reasoned in my mind that the internship could wait until I was ready to walk down that path. They told me I was special, and, if that was true, "special" doesn't simply expire.

Part of me also reasoned that, if these people were willing to pay me a six-figure salary fresh out of law school, what was I really worth? I wanted to push the envelope.

Selling myself short wasn't as attractive as carving a path for myself. So, I took the long way just to get here.

My professional career has turned into a 20-year journey; one that was predicated, in some part, on being indoctrinated to assume that I was valuable.

When they told me I was special, I believed them!

I may have struggled to recognize the value in myself, but I didn't have any problem reading between the lines. This doesn't mean that my decision was easy in any way. I often experienced moments of doubt, times when I questioned my decision to venture out on faith. Each time, I had to remind myself of the value the world saw in me before I ever recognized it. To this day, I repeat the mantra: "You are special. You *can* get this done."

Professor Ogletree was the perfect confidant. He respected my position and proposed an idea that would help me explore my limits while pushing my passion even further.

Upon his suggestion, I met with one of the school's guidance counselors. A wise African man, slim-built and very accommodating, said with a raspy tone, "So, you are interested in opportunities in Africa?"

Yes.

Yes, I was.

Professor Ogletree mentioned something called the Kenya Human Rights Commission. I went to the guidance counselor eager to offer my services. Before agreeing to reach out to its officials, the counselor checked with me once again; looking over the brim of his glasses, he asked, "And you do know that there is no pay for this assignment?"

I could see the confusion on his face. He was probably used to meeting with students who were frustrated over merely earning a $100,000 salary while their roommate inked a quarter-million-dollar deal. I'm sure it wasn't every day that he met with a student like me.

I told him I was aware of the compensation—or lack thereof. Then, he asked another question in his follow up, "You do know that you will have to purchase your own plane ticket?"

Once again, I told him 'yes'.

Shaking his head in dismay, the counselor did manage to offer a silver lining. He informed me that there was a chance that I could be afforded housing during my stay. And, just like that, I was about to be on my way.

Remarkably, I am sitting on a plane right now, writing this message from high in the sky. Even now, years later, I am overcome with the same nervousness, the same vulnerability as I had then. That trip called for me to venture into a "great unknown." For some reason, I had decided to pass on a life-changing opportunity to work at, what could potentially be, one of the world's greatest law firms. I turned my back on the chance to make money I could only dream about. I was as uncertain as I was sure. I was as determined as I was confused. My mind was flooded with questions like:

"Am I making a mistake?"

"Am I just being stubborn, or do I really believe in what I'm doing?"

I felt foolish—just plain dumb. Even still, I never changed my mind. Despite the allure of what most would claim was the "rational" decision, my spirit could not settle on the idea of working at a law firm. If I went against my personal beliefs, I felt like I would be betraying myself. For me, honoring my truth was more important than the title and the perks—and the paycheck. (It still makes me cringe, though!)

Shortly after our talk, I received the news of an opportunity to intern at the Kenya Human Rights Commission in Nairobi, Kenya. The offer was placed on the table, but there were just a few small details for me to attend to. Details that weren't so small when I really dug into them.

Obstacle #1: Where was I going to get $1,000 for a plane ticket to Africa?

Obstacle #2: I didn't know much about the area or the culture; how was I going to cover basics like finding (and *paying for*) food?

Obstacle #3: Will there be a place for me to sleep when I get there?

But I was special, right? I shouldn't have had any problem with figuring things out.

(Please be informed that I am crying and laughing inside right now...)

Well, when I heard the news, it just so happened that my father had a rather stable tree cutting business. All of my siblings had left the nest, except one of my younger sisters. I weighed my options and considered asking the unthinkable.

If you remember from any of my previous stories, we weren't the wealthiest family on the block. Even though $1,000 was not an overwhelming sum, and I was sure that my parents did not have it "sitting around the house" but could manage to find provision as they always had, it still took a lot for me to muster up the courage to ask.

To be clear, I had zero dollars of my own. If my parents did not offer to cover my airfare, then I was going to be out of luck.

Fortunately, they agreed to purchase my ticket to Kenya. They even sweetened the deal by giving me $200 in pocket money! That meant a lot to a struggling first year law student with hopes of changing the world on his own.

Now, I was off with a new mission: Nairobi or Bust—June 1995.

My bags were packed, the heaviest of my belongings being my "fear." On my way to the airport, the only contact I had was a name someone from the foundation had given me and a promise that this man would be there to meet me when I landed.

My plane landed in Kenya at around 1 a.m. I couldn't really take in the sights, since the early morning hours covered the sky in a blanket of darkness. I do remember being taken aback by the airport; it was nothing like anything I'd experienced in the past. I'd never visited a third world country before. As soon as I touched down, I had to manage my first world expectations. I'd become accustomed to airports run by modernized operations. As soon as I arrived, I saw that Nairobi would be an adjustment.

Fortunately, I was not alone. Before I placed my foot on the ground, I heard my name called out from the distance. My contact was there waiting, as promised. After asking me about the flight, he confidently led me out into the darkness.

All I remember was "black." Amidst the darkness, I could barely make out the road. I could identify the faint silhouette of cars and saw evidence of a vast landscape, but that was it. No buildings. No homes. Just space.

As we approached his car, he made the first confession; one of my fears had come true. "We have not figured out accommodations for you yet. There's a hotel in town, however. It is safe and not that expensive. Do you have $20?"

That pocket money was coming in handy already.

On our ride, I learned that the gentlemen who picked me up from the airport was actually a director at the Commission. He told me that he attended Harvard for his master's degree and, as it turned out, he was good friends with the counselor from the Law School who helped me.

We rode along a dirt road for a while before pulling up in front of a small, dark hotel. With only four or five steps leading to the entrance, I made my way towards the clerk waiting in the lobby, paid for a room, and, just like that, I was alone. There was a chill in the air. The room was just large enough for a twin bed and not much more. I could almost stretch out my arms and touch the walls. The room was pitch black. Again, it was my military experience that made the room, the darkness, and the unknown, ordinary. It was the defining moment of being able to find comfort in my discomfort. I had a set of headphones and a Walkman. Knowing me, I probably had Prince in rotation as I drifted off to sleep.

The director promised to return to pick me up at 8 o'clock in the morning. I was awakened to a new world that morning, figuratively and literally. I walked down the stairs I had walked up several hours earlier. I arrived to chilled darkness, and I was greeted in the morning by the warmth and brightness of the sun and the proud people of Kenya. Unbeknownst to me, the next six weeks would sculpt the direction of the rest of my life. I made my trip to Kenya in 1995, while the country was under the leadership of a dictatorial regime headed by President Daniel Moi. Kenya was attempting to heal from the effects of tribal-related conflicts between the Kikuyu and Luo tribes. From the outside looking in, the nation was handling their affairs most notably.

As an intern at the Kenya Human Rights Commission, I assisted in drafting provisions to be presented for inclusion or amendment in the Kenyan Constitution. That was my day job. I spent my evenings and weekends visiting the local market. From the first time I laid my eyes on the market, I was mesmerized by its cultural display of craftsmanship. Paths were lined by vendors manning carts adorned with goods that were expertly made by native nationals. Before long, I learned that Kenyans were not only friendly, they were incredibly resourceful. In the market, there were plates made of soapstone; earrings made from coconut shells and banana peels; paintings; and malachite, hematite, and lapis—precious stones strung together as necklaces and bracelets.

Caught up in amazement, I spent hours at the market every day. I was hypnotized by the daily display of skill, dexterity, creativity, vibrancy, and entrepreneurial zeal. I saw the market as more than a way of life or a means to an end. It was a representation of who they were as a people, a representation of their culture—their heritage.

The market was a firsthand display of the power that can come from merging commerce and cultural road mapping. I noticed the way this natural display of artistry attracted people from all over the world. Every day, visitors, myself included, would flock to the market to marvel at how talented and gifted the locals were.

Then, a lightbulb went off. I decided to send samples of the jewelry to my mother. I wanted her to take the jewelry to her job and tell me how her co-workers responded.

I wanted to see if they were as mesmerized as the rest of us were. There was only one issue. I *still* didn't have any money.

Well, what kind of "special" person would I be, if I were to allow a little inconvenience like money stop me? I got inventive and revised my strategy. After all the time I'd spent at the market, I had built some rich relationships with a few regular vendors. I decided to ask some of my friends if they were willing to advance me a few pieces. And, they did.

Before I was done, I managed to assemble approximately 50 pairs of earrings, assorted necklaces, and bracelets on contingency. Ready to test my hunch and see if the loan was worth the effort, I mailed the jewelry off to my mother using UPS. I probably paid about $50 out of pocket for the shipping, a nominal investment for what would hopefully become a lucrative new business.

Anxiously awaiting a response from my mother, turned makeshift market researcher, I was on edge. When I finally received her report, everything went as expected. Her co-workers absolutely loved the jewelry. In fact, I think she may have sold a few pieces the very same day.

From that moment, it was official. My first formal business was born during the summer of 1995 in the bustling market off Nairobi, Kenya.

Well, it was born in theory. I managed to bypass it for a while, but my problem resurfaced again. I didn't have the money to scale up the business like I wanted.

By the time August arrived, it was time for me to return to Chicago. Approaching summer's end, I only had about two weeks before my second year of law school was set to begin. Rather than focus on the second round of educational politics, I took that hiatus as two weeks for me to figure out how to get my business up and running.

I had all the most important variables in place: connections in Africa, knowledge of the product, and an identified market that was interested in the goods. In my mind, I felt like I could ramp up my business model to mirror the mechanics of well-known brands like Mary Kay. The plan was to hire a team of independent contractors to sell jewelry at birthday parties, jewelry parties, festivals, and the like. I was prepared to create a business that would intrinsically benefit all involved, from the vendors at the market to the independent contractors, and, of course, myself.

This became my official plan to escape Corporate Law Firm "sentencing".

Before ironing out the details, I realized that I needed to do some more (official) market research. One day, I took a trip to the local mall to scope out the "competition." I wanted to see if anyone was selling anything as beautiful or unique as the jewelry I "discovered." To my amazement, I could barely find anything that was even remotely similar to Kenya's style.

On my stroll, I discovered something else that caught my eye. I noticed a vacant storefront nestled in the corner, right next door to a well-known department store called Carson Pirie Scott. The idea of having a storefront never occurred to me. I had zero experience in retail. I thought my independent model was foolproof but seeing the store piqued my curiosity.

Willing to take a risk, I decided to inquire about the space. I found a guard and asked him where I could find the management office. Following his direction, I was disappointed to see that just about everyone was already gone. It was a Friday, around 4 pm. I assumed the staff had left to enjoy their weekend.

There was a secretary still lingering around. I walked up to her and asked about inquiring about a vacancy. She told me to call the office on Monday and make an appointment to meet with a retail leasing agent. Figuring I'd done all that I could, I was prepared to just take a card and walk out the door. Then, a booming voice surprised me from behind. Trailing in from his office, the mall manager overheard our conversation and invited me to come in and talk.

Sitting across his desk, the interview commenced:

"So, what are you looking to sell?"

"Jewelry from Africa made from stones, banana peels, cooper, aluminum, coconut shells, and soap stone," I responded.

"You know we sell a lot of jewelry already, don't you?" He offered his rebuttal.

"Yeah, but not like this. It's like nothing you've ever seen before."

Confident in how "special" this jewelry was, I offered to show him a few samples on the spot. He was interested, so I ran to retrieve the pieces I had in the trunk of my car.

With the product in hand, more questions followed. He asked about my background and experience. He wanted to know if I could follow through.

I shared a few details about my life. I let him know that my father was an entrepreneur, so it was already in my blood. I told him how I came up with the business idea while standing in the middle of a bustling Kenyan marketplace. I also let him in on a few other details like me being on my second year of Harvard Law and a veteran of the US Army.

As fate would have it, he was also a veteran. I think hearing the words "Harvard Law" played to my favor too. He was convinced. Next, he wanted to talk numbers.

"How much of this do you think you can sell?"

With figures dancing through my head, the more we talked, the more I realized the potential that could come from this conversation.

He told me that the mall typically rented spaces for $1,500 per month plus a prorate share of Common Area Maintenance (CAM).

There was no way I could come close to being able to afford that. I had to be honest with him. I needed a fixed rate for rent. I knew I could sell the jewelry, but I couldn't live with the uncertainty of random fluctuations in my share of maintenance.

I guess that first year of law school paid off because I managed to talk him into meeting me somewhere in the middle. His final offer was to rent the space to me for two years at $1,000 per month—solid. Before leaving his office, he looked me in the eye and said, "I'm going to take a chance on you."

A chance—that's all I needed.

Monday, I was back in the office picking up my lease.

Still full of hopeful optimism, with the agreement in hand, I couldn't ignore the fact that I was facing two new dilemmas.

One, I had no money. (Well, that wasn't new. It seemed to be a recurring problem back then...)

And two, in a matter of days I was supposed to be on my way to complete law school in Cambridge, but this store I was opening was in Chicago.

And, remember, I didn't have any money.

Let me pause here to add a disclaimer—folks, please don't try this at home.

There was already a lot on my plate, and, for some reason, I just kept piling things on. The plan was to allocate the money I'd be receiving (i.e., my student loan refund check) towards purchasing merchandise and covering the lease for the store. Knowing I couldn't handle everything on my own, I decided to solicit my old college running mate, James, to join me as a partner. With him on board, I could offset my absence while away at law school and offset costs.

Fortunately, James was all in.

Swallowing my pride and believing in my dream, I went to my parents for one more loan. My mother gave me permission to use her American Express card, putting $1,200 in my honey pot. James rallied up his resources, and I scraped up all that I could. By the time we were done, we managed to pull together about $5,000 to start us off.

My father and a couple of his friends helped us demo the store. We painted and even built a small deck in the back. With our funds, James and I purchased two round trip tickets to Nairobi, so we could pick up some more merchandise. Then, it was time for me to head back to school.

I was only one month into my second year before I was headed back to Kenya to purchase merchandise to stock our store. With $3,000 to spend, we gathered all that we could.

I guess those long hours in the market really paid off. In only a matter of weeks, I managed to build a level of trust with many of the merchants, which allowed them to agree to an unusual opportunity. My offer was a 25–50% deposit on the merchandise, with the balance paid in 60–90 days. Those who accepted the deal were more than happy to see us the next time James and I returned to Nairobi; this time with $10,000 to purchase jewelry and a few pieces of art; we were already expanding, and the business was paying off.

That $10,000 of wholesale jewelry yielded about $50,000 in retail sales. The margins on selling jewelry are extraordinary. We were looking at as much as a 500% percent markup on most of our inventory.

There's a reason why you can find jewelry for sale almost anywhere.

From that Friday when I visited the mall, to the day of the grand opening of my African boutique, Ernest Brandon, only 90 days had passed. After starting with no merchandise and barely any money, we went from concept to open doors in just 90 days!

Our grand opening was on November 25, 1995, just one day before Thanksgiving. Seeing my vision come to life gave me plenty to be thankful for myself. I was twenty-five years of age and I was ready to take on the world.

This stage in my life turned into a tremendous experience that taught me about qualities and principles that would serve me forever.

I learned about the power of building *relationships*; my time in the marketplace wasn't spent as a spectator—I interacted with the merchants. I spoke to them and learned about who they were. My interest was noticed. In the end, those relationships paid off.

I learned about having *integrity*. My word was my bond. I paid every merchant I worked with as promised, which allowed us to grow together.

I learned the importance of being *prepared*. Who knows how that situation could have played out, if I didn't have that jewelry waiting in my trunk? I'm sure the mall manager wouldn't have been as impressed with my story.

I learned about the strength of *credibility*. The mall took a chance on me because I had already proven that I was a man with purpose and conviction. As a veteran and a law student, I was perceived as a person who was trust-worthy and could follow through with their commitment.

As the saying goes, "luck is the intersection of opportunity and preparation". I was very "lucky" on that fateful day in Evergreen Plaza Mall.

You just never know where an experience will lead you. That's why you must always promise to make the most of every moment—you owe it to yourself to do so.

You can't wait for opportunity to fall into your lap. Sometimes, you have to take a risk and place yourself in spaces and places that are new and unfamiliar. The pathways to many of life's greatest lessons and fascinating journeys are behind doors we are too afraid to open. Feel the fear and do it anyway. If you don't take anything else from the exchange, you'll walk away with experience.

I will say this, starting a business is a lot like having a child. No one is really ever fully prepared for it. You can read all the books in the world and perform as much market research as you want, but you'll never *fully* know what you're getting yourself into.

Being an entrepreneur taught me the difference between being "more prepared" and fully prepared; the latter presenting itself like a long-distance myth. This experience, coupled with many years of experience that came thereafter, taught me that the fundamentals of business success are universal.

It doesn't matter what industry you wish to break into, or even if you decide to opt for the job security that comes from corporate settings, you'll need to embody the same essentials:

✓ Relentless Work Ethic
✓ Determination
✓ Interpersonal Skills

- ✓ The Ability to Spot Opportunity
- ✓ Resourcefulness
- ✓ Creativity
- ✓ Confidence
- ✓ Integrity
- ✓ Something to "Play For"—a Goal

As cliché as it may sound, you need to know how to think outside of the box and you need to be a little crazy, if I do say so myself.

My time in retail taught me all I needed to know about marketing, management, point of sale systems, customer service, and merchandising. Believe it or not, all of these skills were transferrable. They continued to serve me when I went on to practice law. I would even go as far as to say that one of my greatest strategic advantages as a lawyer came from the knowledge and experience I gained in retail.

My advice to anyone seeking a breakthrough is to acquire knowledge and skills that are transferable; i.e., people skills, effective verbal and written communication, listening skills, attention to detail skills, system building skills, patience, risk tolerance skills.

Money is important, but in no way do I believe it is the most significant factor in determining a business' success. All things being equal, money becomes the Big Joker in a game of Spades. It moves the meter. I believe that resourceful people find the money, but determined people find the money *and* the way. I firmly believe if I had access to too much capital in the early stages, it would have not been advantageous to my business. Without money, I was forced to learn and earn my relative business success. With money, I may have tried to purchase many of the lessons I was forced to learn, which is a common occurrence.

Ultimately, my partnership with James dissolved after a year or so. In his absence, I continued operating the business on my own. Juggling my responsibilities, I alternated my weekends between Chicago and Cambridge for two more years. I worked at my store during all my breaks and I stayed there every summer. To keep things in motion, I hired one full-time employee to work in the store. Along the way, I also had a few friends and family pitch in. Of course, it was never for free.

With time, I expanded the business to include silver jewelry from Taxco, Guerrero, Mexico. Ernest Brandon evolved into becoming an accessory store filled with jewelry, silver, and shoes. It was quite an adventure.

After graduating from law school in 1997 I continued to work at my two stores full time. My mother thought I was absolutely losing my mind. If I were her, I'd think I was losing my mind too.

Her, "Are you sure? Why would you sell jewelry instead of being a lawyer?"

I'd explain, "I am still going to be a lawyer. I just won't be practicing law. I'll use what I learned in law school to run my business." As If that would make it better.

My father, to his credit, he never broke ranks—at least, not in my presence. He would simply say, "Let the boy do what he wants. When he's ready to be a lawyer, he will."

I did take and pass the bar exam in March 1998. I was still set on NEVER practicing law; much like I was never going to college when I was in high school. A classic case of "how God smiles as Man makes plans for himself."

So, I continued to operate my business and tirelessly work in my store, now expanded to a second location. There was not one day I dreaded going into work. Despite all the days of having negative five dollars in my bank account; employees stealing and quitting without notice; not knowing how I'm going to make payroll at the end of the week—it was still great. Many of the friends I have today, I met at my store. Many of the skills I use in my law practice were sculpted in that business.

1997, 1998, 1999, 2000, I not as much looked at a law book. I made a way to make a respectable amount of money between years three and six (1997–2000). However, by the time 2001 rolled around, I knew it was coming to an end. The soon-to-be deep recession was decimating retail beginning in 2000.

By 2001, I could sense that the end was near. We were already experiencing the effects of the pending recession and, judging by the way retail began to fall apart at the close of 2000, I could tell that things were only going to get worse.

The more the country suffered, I found myself suffering along with them. The hours were getting longer, and the returns were getting smaller. Eventually, I had to question the longevity of my investment. I can recall one point when I was sitting in my store on a Sunday afternoon. Business was slow and I thought to myself, "Maybe I should take a day off." Then, it hit me—I hadn't taken a day off in over three months!

That wasn't even the most impressive part. The fact that I never realized how hard I was working was the thing that really stuck out to me.

The constant joy I had was now being replaced with frustration. That was my sign!

When you don't love what you are doing, even when it's not perfect, it's time to make a change.

I rode the wave of the recession and did my best to stay afloat. Ernest Brandon continued to offer exclusive cultural accessories until February 2012. By then, I had fallen behind on my rent payments. The owner of the mall, whom I had befriended, had no choice but to begin formal eviction proceedings against me. I was in arrears on my rent approximately ten thousand dollars. I packed up both stores and moved all the merchandise to my home. The fixtures were placed in my garage. I sold the remaining inventory from my living room. It was over!

It wasn't an end. It was the beginning of my next chapter. I was failing forward!

Chapter 8

The Great Recession of 2008

"What had happened was..." Whenever a conversation begins with that phrase, you can count on a lie, drama, some bullsh*t, a loan request, or some other unpleasantry to follow. So, what had happened was:

Wall Street came up with their version of a brilliant idea to make even more and easier money than what was being made collecting mortgage interest payments and fees. Who wants to collect hundreds of dollars in interest from struggling homeowners over a thirty-year period? That takes too long.

Instead, they pooled the mortgages together and sold them as securities. I know that sounds like Martian talk to most people. A trust bought up the mortgages and sold them to investors. I mean they sold the mortgages to the investment brokers managing the retirement accounts on behalf of the homeowners whose mortgages were bundled and sold. Essentially, you financed the banks' lending of money to you and were sold your own mortgage. Oh, and you and your co-workers were a bad investment!

It's 2002, my retail store had just closed. My father, who was my hero, suddenly passed away just a few months prior. The country and the world were still enthralled in the aftermath of the tragedy of September 11th. The economy was in a slight pre-recession period, but most were unaware. I had a strong sense of a downward shift in the economy. In retail you feel the effects of market downturns. It was rather clear to me that America was somewhat hemorrhaging in its economy. I had begun investing in real estate in 1998. I persuaded my mother and father to invest in my first purchase. It was a thirty thousand dollar single-family home. I'd invest ten thousand dollars and they'd invest twenty thousand dollars. I'd oversee the rehab; we'd refinance in my name after the property was rehabbed. I'd pay them their investment back along with half the amount of equity. The entire process would take six months. Then, lenders were requiring at least six months seasoning after a change in title to refinance at eighty-five percent of the value. (The loan to value ratio of 85%).

Loan to Value Ratio.

Value of the property after repair	$65,000.00
85% of $65,000.00	$55,250.00
Initial investment return	$30,000.00 (20 to parents, 10 to me)
Rehab costs	$10,000.00
Parents return	$12,500.00 (half of value of equity)
My return	$12,500.00 or 80% return on investment (10k up-front; 5k or 50% of rehab costs)

Sounds like a great plan, huh? Well, about three months into the project my mother had a change of heart. She wanted out. She didn't quite understand why I couldn't just refinance then—prior to six months. She was putting pressure on my father. My father would say, "Just see what you can do. Your mama is driving me crazy." My parents decided they didn't want any profit. They only wanted their investment returned. They'd let me have the house and any remaining equity. I was a bit upset. This was going to be the first of many transactions I would do with my parents. It kinda broke my heart we could not see it through together. I interpreted my mother's stance as not having faith in me. But, I would come to realize many years later, entrepreneurs are not like other people and my mother's "cold feet" was not personal. The fact she took such a risk in the first place speaks volumes of the faith she had in me.

Entrepreneurs are not like other people. Entrepreneurs have a much higher threshold for uncertainty and risk.

It's important you select partners for entrepreneurial endeavors who have the necessary risk tolerance, patience, and confidence in the project and the person managing the project. Otherwise, it doesn't matter how well the investment is proceeding, the emotion of one or more investors or key participants can frustrate the objective. As in the case with my mother, father, and myself, we were able to work it out, thankfully. There's a saying that doing business with family is the toughest. I'm not certain if that is necessarily true. It may be the issue of doing business with a person who does not have the same ideas and tolerance as you more so than it is the family dynamic. I think the error is not solely that it's family; it's that we make the mistake of thinking that because we have a good familial relationship it should also translate into a good business relationship. But, being good together as family is different than getting along in business.

It's not that family is difficult to do business with; it's that you can't do business with all people, and that includes family. You must choose a business partner as carefully as you choose a mate.

I refinanced the property into my name. I paid my parents back all the money they invested. They did not lose a penny. I sectioned off the basement and created a 2-bedroom 1-bath apartment with its own entry and exit. The upstairs was a 2-bedroom 1-bath also. I rented the upstairs for seven hundred and fifty dollars per month. I moved into the basement apartment. My mortgage with taxes and insurance was approximately $650 per month. That was my initial real-world introduction to real estate investment.

For ten years prior to writing this book, I have been on the radio in Chicago, hosting seminars, and participating on panels regarding all matters related to real estate. In 2002, after the closing of my retail stores, I decided to dust off that ole one hundred thousand dollar law degree. I started my law practice from the unfinished bathroom and living room of the upstairs apartment of the property I purchased with my parents' assistance and was in the process of renovating.

At this time, my father had passed, my business had essentially failed, I was in the middle of a rehab, I was broke, and I was starting a law practice; yea, that sounds about right. That is the story of my and many others' lives. Life comes at you fast and from many angles. Question is: how are you going to respond?

I called my sister, LaShawn, who also worked with me for many years at my stores and told her of my next venture. She was on board. The next week she was setup in the barren living room at a small desk and acting as my secretary and paralegal.

I started covering real estate closings for a friend. He paid me seventy-five to one hundred dollars per closing. I'd cover cases for him at seventy-five dollars an appearance. I managed to make a few hundred dollars per week that way. I literally showed up to closings and court with no experience. I'd excuse myself from the room and phone my friend when I had a question. Within one year or so, I had made it up the real estate closing learning curve. I added landlord tenant matters. Then I began incorporating small businesses. Then I read up on something called trusts. I started on the proverbial "fryer" and worked my way up to "Manager" of the store. It took me two years before I developed a basic competency in real estate transactions and landlord tenant law.

In 2005, I integrated more of what I learned in business and in retail: how to market myself and my business. How to market product lines and carve out a niche to drive overall business success. With that I had become the "go to" attorney for a few real estate brokers and loan officers in the area. With their referrals and my marketing in the yellow pages, I was able to begin to carve out a decent living for myself.

I purchased a three thousand square foot former residential foreclosure property. It was formerly used as a daycare center. It was a complete gut rehab. No bank would loan me the money given the condition of the property or my credit. I was introduced to a "hard money" lender and closed the deal in two weeks. It was an interest only loan with a twenty-four month balloon payment.

An interest only loan allows the borrower to pay only the interest for a certain period of time. Interest only loans were designed for investors. The idea is that having to pay only interest frees up cash flow. Greater cash flow helps the investor continue with other projects or "buys them time" while they are in the process of selling or "flipping" the property underlying the loan. A lot of investors got themselves into trouble overutilizing this type of loan product. They either underestimated the time frame it would take to rehab and sell the property, or they were too optimistic in their ability to refinance out of the loan once the underlying property was rehabbed.

I know the story all too well, because I ran into the balloon wall! One would think running into a balloon wouldn't be such a bad thing. I'd imagine a hot summer day. Laughter in the air and red and blue balloons being tossed by one friend to the other. Refreshing sprays of cool water is the only consequence of this balloon! Well, not so with the balloon I'm talking about. This balloon is like a brick wall. It caused nightmares for hundreds of thousands. Adding interest only to the balloon is like mixing the water with a little bleach. Your clothes are ruined. Your skin is burning. You need a chemical warfare team to detox you if you're hit clean.

Welcome to the wild world of 2005 through 2009.

I know this story personally and professionally. When I said in law school, I wanted to be a real estate "expert." Perhaps I should have been a bit more specific on my desired pathway too.

At the same time I was living my nightmare experience, I was representing and seeing more and more clients with exotic loans like the one I had, but much worse!

Interest only, 15% interest rate, fifteen thousand dollars in up-front fees, prepayment penalties, and a twelve month balloon. Hard-money lenders were legalized loan sharks. The access to capital through these loan sharks was everywhere. There was no racial discrimination in their accessibility. Black, white, young, and old alike. Seasoned investors and wannabe investors all joined in.

The hard-money lenders began making so much money, the conventional financial institutions wanted in on it. So, they rolled out their own versions of these loans too: no doc loans. No doc loans are loans that do not require the borrower to submit the customary documentation to the lender for qualification. I mean, silly stuff like proof of income. It was a "we believe you" loan. How much money do you make, Mr. Truth? One hundred and twenty thousand dollars annually, Mr. Shark. Why, that's great. Leave your blood...I mean, please sign here.

In 2006, I wrote a newsletter called, "Crises: Foreclosure." I followed it up with "King Kong Has Nothing on Me: Foreclosure."

I wrote and sent letters to mayors and other elected officials, warning them of the imminent defaults and potential devastation to their communities. Many of the investors were renting the properties. It was only a matter of time before massive defaults would lead to foreclosures. As a real estate attorney, I saw the signs first. I knew the heavy mortgage load many investors were carrying. Going from one hard-money loan to the next with no real plan or profit to support the financial obligation. It was essentially a personal financial Ponzi scheme: using the next loan to service the debt on the prior loan; and so on and so on.

Add to the mix the ungodly number of local loan officers and realtors who turned into expert sheepdogs for the banks. Rounding people up by the droves. Seminars every weekend on the ease of which they could make millions in real estate and retire in 3 years. "Here ye, here ye. Step right up. I can show you how to take the fifty thousand dollars equity you've built up over twelve years in your home and make one million dollars in a matter of twelve months." They did this to aunts, uncles, cousins, sisters, brothers, mothers, and fathers. Everyone was seemingly drinking the magic juice.

At the top of this Mountain of Chaos sat the Banksters! The Banksters, aka Wall Street, saw real opportunity. Not single-family home variety opportunity. Not retire with a real estate portfolio cash flowing ten thousand dollars a month opportunity. That's barely lunch money. The Banksters saw Billion Dollar opportunity! I mean Trillion Dollar opportunity. The Big T; suckas. You gotta say "suckas" in Flava Flave's voice. It's a dragging uuuuuuuuuuhhhh-hhhhs. Like: Suckuuuuuuuuhhhhhhhhhhs!

So, all great American tales involve a villain. Well, reader, meet villain, Wall Street Banks.

Wall Street began expanding their menu of products quicker than McDonald's did during the birth if the health food craze. You want Interest Only? No problem. You want No Document Loans? No problem. You want Stated Income Loans (You simply STATE your income—they believe you)? No problem. You want a low introductory interest rate? No problem. Adjustable Rate Mortgages to the rescue. You only need the loan for a while? No problem. Please take this lovely Balloon with you. You were denied access to credit from the local bank we own? No problem. We have a subsidiary company that provides loans to people with credit "challenges." You are a member of a class of people who have historically been denied credit by banks: black and brown people? No problem. We will refer you to our "other" bank to get you all taken care of. No problem. Poor and white and don't know where to find financing? No problem! You can join the black people too.

You want a No Doc, Adjustable Rate Mortgage with a Balloon Payment, no problem! At Wall Street, it is your way, always.

The subprime mortgage market was manufactured and operated by Wall Street from a pure place of greed.

The Wild Wild West had nothing on 2006, 2007, and 2008.

Welcome to the Great Recession of 2008

"All things that go up, must come down." And, this one came down hard.

Middle America lost much of the security it had built financially in the equity of their homes. Wall Street faked a sprained ankle and was supplied with a trillion dollar bailout by the Government. They called it too big to fail. The idea was that if some of these banks folded the repercussions would be too devastating to the economy. So as comedy would have it, the Banksters were given money to help them recover from the fallout they masterminded and manipulated. That's like me breaking into your home, stealing your most prized possessions, having my car break down halfway along my getaway path, and having the police tow me to the getaway garage. I am a great father; I work at a school and take care of my mother. All in the community where I commit these burglaries. I'm too significant to fail. I'm going to try that reasoning next opportunity I get. Ok, it's not quite the same, but you get the point. The irony of it.

Well, all was not lost. Homeowners were given hope in the name of the Home Affordable Modification Program (HAMP). It was designed to assist homeowners struggling to pay their mortgage. The banks who accepted funds from the government were required to participate in the rebuilding of the "homes" they helped "destroy." Fine, I'll shut up about it soon! I just can't seem to get over this!

This is where I come in. In late 2008, early 2009, the foreclosure crises I attempted to warn people about began ravaging America. I went from two or three foreclosure clients to 100 almost overnight. Then 200. People were in a complete panic. The courts were not equipped to handle the caseload or prepared to address the legal issues presented in these cases. The HAMP Guidelines were adopted by the banks and conferred some protections to the homeowner. I filed thousands of Motions on behalf of defaulting homeowners in the Court. In fact, I believe I was the first to incorporate a HAMP defense in a Motion to Stay a Sale in Cook County. The law was evolving literally overnight.

The banks were overwhelmed by the hundreds of thousands of requests for assistance. Paperwork was lost. Applications would go unanswered for months. In the belly of this storm were hard working people who were oftentimes victims of their own thirst to participate a bit more in the American Dream. It was the retired government worker who took a bet on himself as an investor and was now faced with losing it "all." It was grandma and grandpa who supported their grandchild's dream of building a real estate investment business and so they refinanced the home they had paid off years prior and invested it in a six-flat that is now in foreclosure.

Oh, not so fast. How about the people who didn't do any of that? They invested money in their pensions and stocked away dollars in their annuity. That's it. How did they get entangled in this mess? Well, remember, the Banksters do not discriminate. Trillions of dollars were invested in the securities created by the banks and supported by the bad mortgages sold into the market. It was sort of like what parents would say years ago, "if I come home, and something is broken, everyone is in trouble!" Yea, this one included everyone! Whether you had some direct role or participation in it or not.

I spent ten years fighting on behalf of homeowners to keep their homes. What I found was something much greater than bricks and mortar were at stake for many. Their dignity was implicated. The preservation of years of memories were at stake. An encroachment of their sensibility of right and wrong was being disrupted. Their belief of a just and fair America was being challenged. The trust many struggled to maintain with the government was frustrated.

The 99%s! The very fabric of America was being pulled at. Not just at home, but abroad also.

This was a time in the History of America and the world we should never forget.

It is a story of over-optimism and rushing to "fools gold" for many of us. It is the reality that many who were trusted to act in the best interest of their neighbors, did not. Realtors, lawyers, loan officers, title company owners, and other trusted professionals were complicit in the breakdown. The Banksters and their greed emerged as a dark sinister cloud, seeming to disregard everything and everyone with the exception of their personal profit—including the issue of corporate responsibility, fiduciary duty, conflicts of interest, and the efficacy of allowing banks to engage in investment banking.

Strangely, the banks have made record breaking profits in the aftermath. At the end of the first quarter of 2010, First American CoreLogic estimated that 24% of mortgages were "underwater."

As of 2019, we are still digging ourselves from under the destruction of the Great Recession.

My motivation and responsibility in writing this book is in my adherence to the karmic principle of "to whom much is given, much is required."

I found my story in the story of the thousands of homeowners I have assisted in saving their homes. And in the handful that were not as fortunate. The stories must be told. In Africa, history is preserved around the fire as the elders tell the stories of the ancestors. From those stories we are informed of our character and of our possibilities. We are provided a roadmap upon which to follow, refine, and build upon.

As we venture into the next cycle, it is my ambition to be a beacon of possibility. To educate and inform the 99%s. To prepare us for what may be, or what is, to come. The next great financial and social "crises" or challenge I estimate to be the Student Loan crises and the "living too long" dilemma. Remember: that good problem. I want to provide a buffer for what is to come. Good news is: We've been here before. And, we're prepared. You have everything you need!

What's next?

1. Please educate yourself on real estate investment and ownership.
2. Start slow.
3. Partner with a team of professionals (lawyers, financial planners, insurance brokers, and bankers) after interviewing them extensively and checking their references.
4. Investing in real estate or any other business should not be looked upon as a get rich overnight opportunity (and if it looks to good to be true, it probably is!).
5. Play a long game (success in any endeavor is typically created over time).
6. One or two investment properties can change the life of you and your family.
7. Have fun!
8. Invest in excellence, and do not expect perfection.
9. Guard your space from energy drainers and dream thieves. Time is your most valuable asset: make every moment count and account for every moment.
10. Embrace Failure (experience). Be certain to Fail Forward after experience/failure.

Chapter 9

"Do Not Lose Hope: Trust!"

A plan is not a plan unless it is written; a plan that is not written is just a dream.

What do you tell the parents after their healthy seventeen-year-old son has been involved in a life-changing accident? One day, he is a vibrant young man. The world is his canvas with all the beauty of the colors of life's rainbow available to him. For Mr. and Mrs. Murphy and their son, life was good. They had purchased a home in a suburban community outside of Chicago. They had previously lived on the Southside of Chicago. Like so many other loving parents, they desired a better life for themselves and their children. The suburbs of Chicago have been a welcome refuge for many from what is the comparatively fast-paced environment of city life in Chicago. Then what do you say to the wife after the husband suddenly dies on top of all of this?

I wasn't provided many details. My introduction into their lives was by way of their family friend. The conversation went like this:

"Attorney Fenton, I am contacting you on behalf of my friend. I'm really concerned that she is going to lose her home," she said. "Not because she doesn't have the money to pay the mortgage. She is just depressed, and I don't believe she is opening her mail. Her son is nineteen years old. He was involved in an accident about two years ago. He is now paralyzed and requires around the clock care."

I listened and then said, "Wow. I am really sorry to hear that. There are a few things we can do to ease her mind."

"Well, now, it's not just her son. Her husband has recently passed suddenly!" Susan said.

How do you assist a wife and mother facing these challenges?

This is an example of the hardships many are facing. My day consists of attempting to provide financial and legal solace to people on a daily basis while they are mourning the sickness or loss of someone they love. It can be heart-wrenching, but these people need my help while they are going through such terrible difficulties.

I thought about this poor woman. As if it wasn't enough to see your son's life change so dramatically, now she was having to deal with the sudden passing of her husband of twenty plus years.

In December 2018, I met Mrs. Murphy personally. She was fortunate to have a friend who not only took the initiative to phone me on her behalf, but to also literally chauffeur her to my office and hold her hand while she cried and shared her story with me.

Mrs. Murphy was in her late forties and her husband was in his early fifties when he passed. They were both professionals and gainfully employed. They had two children. The eldest child was in college. The youngest child was involved in an accident and now had special needs.

There were some complications with treatment at the hospital her son was taken to after the accident. It was believed the doctors made errors with his treatment. Consequently, a lawsuit was filed (and is still pending as of the publishing of this book).

Mrs. Murphy's mother was recently retired; she sacrificed by moving in almost immediately after the accident. She cared for her grandchild while the parents continued to work. Just as they were adjusting to their new reality and getting in the swing of caring for their child, Mr. Murphy suddenly passed.

Mrs. Murphy said to me, "Attorney Fenton, I don't know what I am going to do. I don't know if I want the house. I really don't know my rights. I'm really concerned about my son. What if something happens to me? My mother is up in age."

At this point, she was completely distraught, and the tears were flowing. Not too long before this meeting, I had watched a very good friend lose her husband, who was also a friend of mine. I have also experienced the loss of my father at the relatively young age of fifty-four. I, too, have vivid memories of the pain of my mother having to bury a man she had spent more than thirty years of her life beside.

Mrs. Murphy's angel of a friend, Susan, handed her a tissue from the box on the edge of my desk to wipe her tears. She reached over and rubbed her back as if to say, "It will be alright." Susan was a former client and frequent listener of my radio broadcast. She helped explain the situation in more detail. Not only was Mrs. Murphy not opening any mail but she was also uncertain if her name was included on the mortgage with her husband. She didn't even know if she was paying the mortgage.

I spoke up, "Mrs. Murphy, I am sorry to hear about your loss. I can't imagine what you are experiencing, but I can say, I can help relieve you of a bit of your burden. I am almost certain you will leave here with a much better understanding of your options regarding your home. Also, we can make certain your son is looked after if something happens to you."

Just with those words alone, I watched as she breathed a sigh of relief.

It was very obvious that she was in deep mourning over the loss of her husband and living in fear of the idea of something happening to her and not knowing what would become of her son.

The first step in resolving a problem, is identifying the problem. Sometimes, the problem is multi-tiered.

I took out a blank piece of copy paper and took notes and drew diagrams as I spoke. I like to use paper without lines on it, because in my mind it gives me permission to create without limitations.

I said, "Mrs. Murphy, here's what I'm hearing from you.

1. The House; to stay or not to stay. And, what are your options given you are not on the mortgage?
2. What can we do to make certain your son is taken care of if something happens to you?"

She said, "Yes."

I responded to her. "Okay, great. I can help you with that. We can solve these two things that are keeping you up at night. I am telling you I am certain we can solve those two issues relatively easily."

What I have come to learn is that many of our most pressing problems are not really that complicated; we just do not know how to solve them on our own. Even worse, oftentimes, people with the answers to some very basic questions or problems attempt to mystify the resolution or withhold the information for ransom, almost.

I do not believe in this. I believe in sharing information freely. I share with any potential client. I will share with you everything you need to know. It is my experience in navigating through the knowledge and adapting to the uncertainty of an issue that may require you retaining my services, but I am willing to tell you everything I know about this issue up front.

What to do about the house?

So, on the first sheet of paper I wrote:

THE HOUSE:

1. You are not on the mortgage.
2. What is the value of the home? And, what is the mortgage balance?
3. Are you in foreclosure? If so, what are your options given what you may decide regarding the home?
4. Your options: a. to sell; b. Assume the mortgage; c. Short sale; d. Do nothing.

My handwritten notes and diagrams usually resemble something between an angry second grader's coloring project and the Mona Lisa. Sometimes, I dramatically toss them to the side and start all over. I find that during the process it engages my client and takes people like Mrs. Murphy out of mourning mode for just a moment and helps them imagine making their situation just a little bit better.

I started on a fresh sheet of paper on the top of which I wrote: THE MORTGAGE. I began to draw as I spoke to Mrs. Murphy. "This is a picture of a house. Standing next to the house is the owner. How do I know it's the owner? I know because the owner's name is stated on the Deed of the home which is recorded in the County where the home is located.

"Mrs. Murphy, you and I know, just because you are married, it does not necessarily mean both husband and wife should be listed on the Deed. In fact, I advise my clients against that in most instances, but we'll get to that later.

"An issue with having one spouse on the Deed and not the other is part of the reason you are sitting here: how does a surviving spouse have their name transferred onto the Deed or Title after the other spouse has passed?

"Mrs. Murphy, here is the answer:

1. Probate,
2. Bond in Lieu of Probate, or
3. You don't.

"The answer is right there. I am going to help you make a choice as to one of those answers. I am going to tell you everything you need to know to make the best decision for you and your family."

THE MORTGAGE

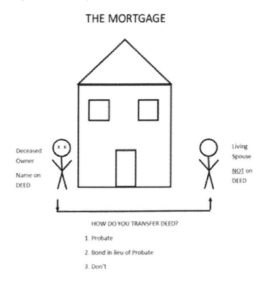

Deceased Owner Name on DEED

Living Spouse NOT on DEED

HOW DO YOU TRANSFER DEED?

1. Probate
2. Bond in lieu of Probate
3. Don't

The big question is:
Do you want to keep your house?

While this might seem like a strange question to some, it is still a very valid one. There might be financial hardship with trying to maintain the house or the emotional need to not have it as a constant reminder of what has been lost. This is the first question that must be answered.

1. YES! I want to keep my house AND I can afford the mortgage.

   We will begin the process of allowing you to keep your home—probate or bond in lieu followed by assumption of mortgage, refinance, purchase, or payoff of mortgage.

2. YES! I want to keep my house BUT I can't afford the mortgage.

   We will begin the process of allowing you to keep your home—probate followed by a short refinance or short sale to yourself.

3. YES! I want to keep my house BUT there was no will and my spouse had children.

   The children automatically inherit half the house. If the children are of age, they will have to disclaim any interest in the home or transfer their interest to you, the surviving spouse. (See Illinois Laws of Intestate Succession Illustration in Workbook)

4. NO! I don't want to keep my house AND there is equity in it.

   We will begin the process of Probate or a Bond in Lieu of Probate to allow you to sell your home.

5. NO! I don't want to keep my house BUT there is no equity in it.

   We can simply choose to DO NOTHING and negotiate with the bank an amount of time you will have to continue residing there until they retake possession after a foreclosure.

In the case of Mrs. Murphy, she was in a position to pursue all available options. There was equity in her home. Her credit had not been damaged to the extent she could not refinance her home from her late husband's name and into her name. She could afford the mortgage and apply for an assumption of the mortgage through the current lender.

The loan was only two months or so behind and she was not in grave danger of losing it to foreclosure. In Illinois a lender cannot even begin foreclosure proceedings until a borrower is ninety days or more behind on their mortgage. And, a borrower, or heir, as in this case, has at least seven months from the time of filing a foreclosure to payoff the mortgage (and that can be done through a sale or refinance).

In the case of Mrs. Murphy, there were no issues with the children. They'd be willing to do whatever was necessary to support their mother's wishes, including transferring their interest in the home and their father's estate to her.

Fortunately, this was not a situation where she was left without sufficient financial resources to care of her family. In total, approximately five hundred thousand dollars in liquid assets were transferred to his wife from savings, retirement accounts, and distributions from insurance policies.

The tragic reality for many is that there will not be sufficient resources to cover the expenses of a traditional burial, not to mention offset the loss of income into the household. The average American household cannot absorb the loss of income from a spouse. The Urban Institute reported the average liquid retirement savings of African Americans was $19,049, Hispanics only $12,329 and Whites $130,472. As of 2018, Northwestern Mutual's 2018 Planning and Progress Study reported, 78 percent of Americans are "extremely" or "somewhat" concerned about having enough money for retirement. The study further provided that 21 percent of Americans have nothing saved for retirement and another ten percent have less than $5,000 saved.

She decided she wanted to keep her home. There was equity. Her son was situated there, along with her mother. She decided to pay the mortgage balance off in full.

Now that we resolved her issue with her home. There was still the anxiety of imagining how her son's life would change if, for whatever reason, she was no longer there to look after him. How would she be certain he'd have a place to live and enough money for the level and quality of care she and her family have been able to provide to that point?

More than anything, this seemed to be the greatest source of her emotions. Since she was left alone after her husband's passing it was up to her alone to ensure their child was protected. She didn't want to let her late husband or their son down. This led us to the second issue we needed to address.

How to Care for a Love One with Special Needs?

The question Mrs. Murphy had is the same as millions of others have:

What do you need to do to make certain your special needs child, disabled spouse, or parent is taken care of if you are no longer able?

My answer always includes, "A Special Needs Trust!"

I told Mrs. Murphy that a special needs trust would preserve her son's eligibility for Social Security Disability benefits and provide supplemental or primary funds for his medical care, housing, food, entertainment, and other day-to-day needs. A special needs trust can be utilized when a person has a physical or mental disability, including those who lack the capacity to manage their own finances.

I reassured her, "When we create the trust it will be drafted according to the specific needs and lifestyle of your son in mind. What level of care do you desire for him? Do you anticipate him remaining in your home or being transferred to a 24-hour care facility? Do you want to make certain to maintain a certain travel schedule or level of extra-curricular activities?"

"In any event, the trust should be created now. You are able to deposit or fund the trust with assets or cash you currently have and direct the transfer of funds in the future to your son's special needs trust. To allow you to sleep a bit better at night, you may decide to fund the special needs trust created for your son with twenty thousand dollars or an amount you estimate would be necessary to supplement the cost of one year of his care. I'm thinking you'd feel a lot better knowing you are prepared in case of an emergency in that way.

"Beyond that, I recommend you purchase an insurance policy in an amount to cover the total costs of the number of years difference between your life expectancy and your son's. If there is a twenty-five year difference in your life expectancy, and an estimated annual cost of care for your son, without your assistance, of fifteen thousand dollars, then after accounting for his income and other assistance, the policy amount should be three hundred and seventy-five thousand dollars.

"Given your relatively young age and medical condition, that will cost you approximately sixty-five dollars per month. At your current age of forty-eight with a life expectancy of seventy-five, I'd recommend purchasing a 30-year term policy, at the very least. In this way, you will not be relying on the money you have now and will earn in the future."

Mrs. Murphy's eyes lit up. She said, "Wow. I never thought about that. I can just purchase additional insurance."

"Yes!" I told her.

An answer so obvious to many escapes the majority of us who fail to see or understand the value of insurance in planning for the long-term well-being of our loved ones.

"Mrs. Murphy, now remember, the funds from this insurance policy will not be given directly to your son. The special needs trust will be the beneficiary of the policy. Upon your demise the insurance monies will be paid to the special needs trust. You will name someone to manage the money and other assets on behalf of your son. This person is called a successor trustee. The trustee's job is to use the trust assets to purchase necessities for your son. They can buy services and products like home furnishings, cover medical and dental expenses, physical therapy, education, vacations, and home furnishings."

"The trustee will initially be you. If you were ever to be incapacitated or upon your expiration, your successor trustee will step up. The successor trustee can be a friend or family member. The successor can be one or more individuals acting as co-trustees. The trustee can even be a company that provides trust services."

I always get a laugh with this: "Trusts have always been around. It's just many of us were not aware. In Chicago, there's a well-known bank called Seaway Bank and Trust. There's also Northern Trust Bank. Many people, including myself for many years, never really stopped to think or ask the meaning of the Trust in the name. Most people just thought Trust in the name meant, 'Trust us!'"

Almost everyone laughs because at one point or another most had that thought.

"The 'Trust' is for the trust services or department that exists at the institution. The trust may last for the duration of your son's life or until funds are depleted. The rich and well-off have been 'trusting' for hundreds of years in America, while the middle class and poor have been only 'banking.' While the more astute of the middle class open bank accounts early on for their children, the rich have been setting up trusts for their children and their children's children."

"Also, any monies from the settlement of your lawsuit can be deposited into the special needs trust. If your son passes prior to the funds in his trust being depleted, you can instruct where the remaining funds will be directed or who will be the successor beneficiary of the trust. In your case, Mrs. Murphy, you may want to instruct the trustee to distribute any remaining funds to your surviving children or grandchildren.

"The bottom line is this, we can make certain a plan is in place along with the resources or cash to ensure the execution of the plan with a special needs trust. A special needs trust preserves the eligibility for government assistance such as Social Security Income, Medicaid, and subsidized housing. If you were to leave money to your son directly, he could lose benefits he may need and qualify for in the future; not to mention he may not have the experience or maturity to manage assets efficiently.

"So, although your oldest son may not have the physical restrictions of your youngest son, it is recommended you set up a revocable living trust with a separate trust provision for your oldest son as well. The revocable living trust is for your benefit while you are living. It shields your ownership of certain property. It provides a mechanism for your money and other assets to be managed on your behalf if you were ever to become incapacitated. It allows you to transfer remaining assets within the trust to your children or retain certain assets in the trust for the management and benefit of your children, just as the special needs trust provides. And, if you like, we can even create a trust provision for your grandchildren.

"Imagine the trust as a person. You are the creator. It is your job to name the trust. The same as you and your husband named your children. The world knows your children by name, but the government identifies your children by a number (a Social Security Number). Well, we will obtain a number from the government for your trust too. It is called an Employer Identification Number. So, the same as a child. It is birthed by you (created), given a name, and issued a number by the government.

"This is where it gets a bit more interesting. With a child, you can never be quite certain of their pathway through life. What's great about a trust is you get to decide in advance what the trust can and cannot do. You get to say who the trust will benefit. You get to decide when. The life cycle of the trust is created by you. Let me put it all together for you."

I grabbed another blank sheet of paper and I drew a circle. Then I pointed to it.

"This circle represents the universe of your trust. I'm just waiting on you to name it. After the trust is created, we will begin to give it 'life' or funding.

1. We will transfer title from your husband's name directly into the trust;
2. We will choose a bank or other financial institution to open a Trust Bank Account to deposit long-term funds into;

3. We will contact insurance and investment brokers and change the beneficiary designation to the trust, as applicable."

(Please see attorneyernestfenton.com for a more detailed explanation and illustration of Trusts)

An hour-and-a-half after she entered my office, Mrs. Murphy left empowered, knowing what steps she was going to take. The tears of relief that she shed reinforced for me that it is a privilege to be able to help her and others when they're going through tough times.

In the end, we created a full estate plan for Mrs. Murphy. A Revocable Grantor Trust with a Pour-over Will for Mrs. Murphy's benefit and her family. A Special Needs Trust for the benefit of her special needs child. And, a Health Care and Property Power of Attorney to complete the plan. Unfortunately, Mrs. Murphy's case is not unusual. On a daily basis I assist individuals and their families navigate life's challenges. This chapter represents an evolution of skills, education, personal development, experience, and consciousness for me. I never imagined I'd be practicing law; I still chuckle at the idea of me being a lawyer. In fact, I still resist the characterization. Where I am, and what I do, is an expression of who I desire to be and how I desire to "show up" in the world. It is my giving back to the Universe some of what it has given me. It is, too, a stop along the pathway of my journey to continued self-discovery and expression of possibility.

It is never simply a question of "what you do," it is a question of "who you be being when you do what you do."

Dedication

This book is dedicated to all the people who poured into me. Most notably, my mother and father, Ruby Mae Fenton and, my hero, the late Ernest James Fenton aka Red. To my wife, Marissa T. Fenton, whom I still cannot believe married me. She has brought new meaning to my Life. To my brother and sisters, other family, and friends who accompanied me along this journey at various stages. This book is also dedicated to the underdog, the written off, the forgotten about, the overlooked, the poor, the forgotten middle class, and anyone else who has good reason to say "'F' the Odds."

I must also acknowledge my writing Editor, Tiara Butler, for her invaluable contribution in lending her writing expertise to this one-year endeavor. She "got" my humor and vision and rolled with it beautifully. Also, special thanks to Wes Cowley for proofreading, formatting, and adding the finishing touches to the book. Thanks to my technical and media guru, Vaughan Smith, the favorite son of Ms. Smith (yes, from the "McDonald's story"), for making certain I advance with the times. And thanks to the father and son duo, JV Cook Sr. and Jr., for making it alright to judge this book by its cover.